# Biometrics in Support of Military Operations

## Lessons from the Battlefield

# Biometrics in Support of Military Operations

## Lessons from the Battlefield

William C. Buhrow

CRC Press
Taylor & Francis Group
Boca Raton London New York

CRC Press is an imprint of the
Taylor & Francis Group, an **informa** business

CRC Press
Taylor & Francis Group
6000 Broken Sound Parkway NW, Suite 300
Boca Raton, FL 33487-2742



Printed on acid-free paper
Version Date: 20161004

International Standard Book Number-13: 978-1-4822-6021-2 (Hardback)



**Library of Congress Cataloging-in-Publication Data**

Buhrow, William C., 1961-
Biometrics in support of military operations : lessons from the battlefield / William C. Buhrow.
pages cm
Includes bibliographical references and index.
ISBN 978-1-4822-6021-2
1. Military intelligence--United States--Methodology. 2. Biometric identification--United States. 3. United States. Army--Personnel management--Data processing. I. Title.

UB251.U5B85 2015
355.4'1--dc23 2015006877

**Visit the Taylor & Francis Web site at**
**http://www.taylorandfrancis.com**

**and the CRC Press Web site at**
**http://www.crcpress.com**

# CONTENTS

# FOREWORD

Biometrics continues to make major contributions to the way United States and Coalition military forces conduct antiterrorist and counterinsurgency operations around the world. In two major theaters of war, Iraq and Afghanistan, as well as in the Global War on Terror, biometrics has proven not only to be a critical enabler for forces needing to positively identify enemy personnel on the battlefield, but also a discrete capability to interface with an otherwise amorphous civilian population. The ability to positively discriminate innocents from those intending to do harm, in real time, is a unique and essential requirement for Coalition forces in the future.

Our recent military history is replete with instances in which biometrics was the single most critical facet leading to success. Since 9/11, the expansion, growth, and focus of biometrics have been dynamic. In their 2004 campaign to take the city of Fallujah, U.S. Marines used biometrics to positively identify captured insurgents during the battle, as well as those who were authorized to draw water and rations after the city had been neutralized. Biometrics quickly became the single most important enabler to their operations at the time. The U.S. Air Force has used biometrics as the centerpiece of base-entry security for the past decade, and U.S. Army forces have utilized a mix of biometric devices and databases for everything—from interdicting the flow of foreign fighters across international borders, to internment and interrogation operations, to the positive identification of individuals hoping to vote in the Iraq and Afghan presidential elections. For the past ten years, near-real-time identity management through biometrics has been a keystone to the successful prosecution of Maritime Interdiction Operations (MIO) by U.S. and Coalition navies against Yemeni pirates and along the Makran Coast. During almost five years as the Senior Intelligence Officer (J2) for the United States Central Command, from 2003 to 2007 I was able to see firsthand how difficult it was for our forces to distinguish friend from foe, particularly in the early days of the Iraqi occupation, and how important the use of biometrics and associated intelligence functions became in our ability to provide precise analysis of the threat, and to more effectively target that threat, while minimizing the effect on the surrounding civilian populace. Had we possessed a comprehensive and well-coordinated biometrics capability during those early days of Operation Iraqi Freedom, it is quite possible that the large-scale detentions of military-aged males that eventually led to the Abu Ghraib crisis and the Iraqi insurgency might never have happened.

However, despite the successful use of biometrics across the spectrum of military missions during the past decade, our ability to apply this knowledge in future operations is jeopardized by the inability to institutionalize biometrics as a capability across the Joint Force. Part of this gap is the result of increasing financial pressures, which are certain to worsen in the coming years as the Services stand down somewhat from a decade of high-paced constant combat operations. But it is also because of a general failure to document the biometrics battlefield lessons learned or to develop a Joint vision and doctrine that would serve as a foundation for developing the capabilities required for future success.

This is where Bill Buhrow's book plays a crucial role in bridging the gap between what we have today and where we and our allies need to go in the future. I have known Bill for more than twenty-five years, since we worked together in operations across the Pacific while assigned to the Army's 125th Military Intelligence Battalion at Schofield Barracks, Hawaii. I know from those experiences and from our continued association over the past two decades that he is the right person to shoulder this project. Bill possesses a truly unique perspective on both the operational and intelligence aspects of biometrics, and this perspective makes it possible not only for him to effectively articulate the potential of current biometrics capabilities, but also to describe a vision for the capabilities our nation will require in the future. Biometrics, as a battlefield capability, had a huge impact on two regional conflicts as well as on the global war against terror, and they will continue to be critical to future military operations, whether they come in the shape of peacetime contingencies, humanitarian operations, or a return to large-scale military operations. As such, I urge those who would lead the way to the military biometrics enterprise of the future to read this book.

John M. Custer
*Major General, Retired*
*United States Army*

# PREFACE

## WHY DID I WRITE THIS BOOK?

I first became involved in biometrics in 2007 after spending the previous 24 years in a variety of intelligence positions in and out of uniform. At the time, I was working in the Army G-2 (intelligence staff for the U.S. Army headquarters) having returned to uniform as an active duty reservist in the fall of 2003. After four years of shift work producing briefing slides for the Army leadership, I decided it was time for something new that would take me out of my comfort zone a bit and possibly lead to a new set of skills. The Army at the time was providing mostly provisional manpower support to something called the Biometrics Task Force (BTF), and my office had supplied a number of folks on short-term, temporary assignments to the BTF. I decided to offer my services for at least a year, which eventually turned into almost five and a new career as a "biometrician."

I often tell people that one of the great things about biometrics is that since it is still new and not yet widely understood, it takes a relatively short amount of experience to be able to claim "subject matter expertise." My first few years at the BTF were spent working on the operational specifications (known as "requirements" in the military) for the future biometrics database and handheld biometrics collection system of the Department of Defense (DoD) and in running the BTF's external outreach efforts. Both of these positions afforded me a good deal of knowledge about the technical and operational aspects of biometrics, but nothing really made it all fit together in my mind until I volunteered to deploy to Afghanistan over the summer of 2009. There I worked for a former BTF member, Colonel José Smith, who had recently taken command of the organization responsible for running biometrics operations across the country. Although I was only there for a few months, I worked on a wide range of issues—from biometrics intelligence support, to biometrics collection on the border, to force protection and policy development. I also learned more about how biometrics are really used in the field and how the biometrics collections and operational usages are supported (sometimes poorly) by the strategic systems and capabilities with which I had become quite familiar back in the BTF.

This experience also revealed to me how the U.S. military often failed to make the best use of the potential of biometrics due to a lack of effective training and education, particularly at the leadership level, and an almost complete absence of authoritative guidance on how to apply biometrics capabilities in support of combat operations. It also showed me that the systems we employed in the field, as well as the communications links and mechanisms we used to send biometrics data and related information back to the United States, were not well suited for the Afghan environment, from either an operational or technical infrastructure perspective. I contend, however, that at least some of the technical shortfalls our forces experienced could have been overcome with a combination of better and more complete training, well thought out and clearly articulated operational concepts, and more effective prior planning and preparation. I took it upon myself to try addressing some of these shortfalls, beginning while still in Afghanistan and continuing after my return to the United States.

The specific genesis for this book occurred during a conversation I had, while still in Afghanistan, with one of the contractors we employed to train biometrics collection system operators. We were talking about the quality of the collection efforts and the differing value that various units seem to place on using their biometrics systems. I remember asking him whether we provided any kind of documentation to the units whose personnel we trained, and he showed me a small booklet (more like a pamphlet) that listed the steps needed to turn the system on and put it in operation, but there was nothing to tell a soldier or his leaders how (or why) they should use this new and relatively unknown capability that we were placing in their hands. I did some searching to try finding something, anything, that might describe some basic operational concepts, but the only thing I could find was a standard operating procedures (SOP) document produced a few years before in Iraq by the U.S. Marine Corps, and even that was far from comprehensive and not well distributed. I also noticed that the U.S. Army's Center for Combined Arms Lessons Learned (CALL) in Ft. Leavenworth, KS, produced a fairly steady stream of publications, including products called "commander's guides," on a wide variety of subjects but relatively little on biometrics. I was determined to change that shortfall so I contacted a CALL representative on email and we worked out a process for the production of a "commander's guide" for biometrics.

The project took shape over the next few months as I returned to the Biometrics Identity Management Agency (BIMA) and developed the outline, coordinated with other biometrics "stakeholders" across the services, and wrote a major portion of the initial draft. I moved on to other duties after that, but my BIMA colleagues, most notably Retired Army Special Forces Officer Mike Kershner, kept the project moving forward, and it was finally published in April 2011. Since then, the "Commander's Guide to Biometrics in Afghanistan" has been well received and widely distributed in both hard copy and online versions, but it is still not as comprehensive as I would like, nor is it readily available to allies or other U.S. Government (USG) personnel outside of DoD. My hope is that this publication will bridge that gap and better educate leaders inside and outside the U.S. military on the far-reaching potential for biometrics in support of tactical operations

## ABOUT THE BOOK: FORMAT, CONTENT AND STRUCTURE

If you are looking for a "How To" manual for military biometrics this is not really the book for you. I'll leave it to the individual organizations and the Services to describe how to execute military identity operations. This is actually intended to be more of a "What To" kind of book. My intent here is to provide a comprehensive look at how biometrics has been used, and can be used, to support a wide range of military missions. While I won't necessarily cover all of the details behind these various kinds of missions and employments, I will try to provide enough detail so that a reader looking to use biometrics to support operations can develop more detailed processes and procedures for a particular organization. I also intend for the document to help inform the vendor community, so suppliers can develop systems and technical processes that better meet the tactical identification needs of military forces.

The reader will also notice that I have chosen to write in what I hope is a less formal and less technical style than much of what has been published on the general topic of biometrics so far. I did so for a number of reasons. First, I am not really a technical guy. While I have studied this issue long enough and attended enough discussion groups and forums to understand a good bit of the details behind biometrics technology and applications, I am at heart a liberal arts college-produced generalist.

Second, I really intend this product to be useful to operators more than biometrics personnel. As such, I'm trying to describe military biometrics applications in a way that makes sense to the people who will actually employ these capabilities to support their combat operations as opposed to writing a document for the system operators or technicians. It has been my observation over the years that we in the biometrics field have not engaged the various operational communities effectively enough to gain support for expanded biometrics employment across the DoD, and this failure has had a negative impact on our operational effectiveness and on providing a solid foundation for the future. I hope that the style of this book will help make it more usable by the leaders of combat arms organizations and those that support them during operations.

Since the general premise of this book is to provide key concepts for the tactical employment of biometrics, I've highlighted these concepts in each of the main chapters and then again in Appendix A, which provides them all, together, in one place. The reader will notice that my focus is almost exclusively on the employment of biometrics in ground combat and supporting operations. This is in large part because, as a former U.S. Army officer and given most of my personal biometric experience, it is what I know best. I understand that the U.S. Navy has also employed biometrics for identification purposes during maritime interdiction operations as well as for overseas facility access control, but the uses are very similar to those employed by soldiers and marines, even if the environment is different. Therefore, I hope this book is also useful to any readers who approach the topic from a nautical perspective as well.

Another technique I've employed to illustrate some of my points is to provide a series of scenarios, beginning with Chapter 3 and continuing through Chapter 7, which highlight the employment of biometrics capabilities in support of specific missions.* Some of these are loosely based upon actual events and others are merely plausible scenarios designed to address a particular set of operational concepts. I hope that these biometric storylines make the concepts I'm discussing "come alive" a bit.

A note about source material—there isn't much. As I alluded to earlier, one of the main reasons I took on this project was the absence of authoritative guidance on the tactical use of biometrics within the DoD. I also believe that the reason my publisher agreed to take on the project is the lack of any similar work in commercial publication. As a result of these publication gaps, the reader will see that my bibliography is rather thin. Where available, I have used the scant official documents regarding

* The scenarios in Chapters 3 through 6 are linked to a central storyline, while the two used in Chapter 7 are separate and distinct.

biometrics, but many of those I'd like to use are labeled "For Official Use Only," and therefore are not really usable. I've also collected and used a number of articles and excerpts from other biometrics and/or military periodicals or web postings and conducted a couple of interviews with people who had somewhat unique perspectives and experiences. But beyond that, most of the contents of the book are from my own personal experiences, my own observations and discussions with colleagues, and my own thoughts.

The structure of this book is also intended to allow the focus to be on biometrics usage rather than on the technology or technical processes. Still, it is useful for even the most knuckle-dragging combat arms leader (no offense meant of course) to have some appreciation for how the biometrics process works, how biometrics modalities compare to each other, and how that can determine the usage and some of the characteristics of biometric systems, so I have included discussions of these topics and others in the appendices.

It is also not my intent for this to be a retrospective on DoD biometrics per se, and I have tried to restrain myself as much as possible from airing my personal frustrations with the Defense Department's biometrics efforts. Where there are positive examples of past biometrics success on the battlefield, I have used them to illustrate key points. However, when necessary, I have also chosen to provide some negative examples of things that were done incorrectly (in my view) or, more often, not done at all. If these examples and my comments strike any readers as excessively harsh, I apologize in advance.

Finally, I am departing a bit at the end of the book (in both the Conclusion and Afterword) from the operational/tactical focus to address issues that are more strategic in nature. The reason is that I believe that biometrics usage in the U.S. Department of Defense is approaching something of a crossroads as the U.S. winds down its large-scale overseas counterinsurgency operations and begins to return to more of a conventional and strategic approach. Put simply, this new environment will not support a biometrics enterprise that is based upon simply doing what we have been doing better but with far fewer resources. This new environment requires a change in the way we develop and maintain the kinds of high-tech and constantly changing capabilities that biometrics represents—and I will address how (I believe) the Army can do this (in Chapter 8). The U.S. DoD also needs to develop a strategic identity capability that incorporates expanded opportunities for biometrics enrollments into our databases by forces in the field. Our new identity system needs to better exploit the massive amount of data that we assemble as part of biometric collections and to use this data to improve our identification operations. I will address these two concepts as well as several others in the Afterword.

Because of my professional background and the nature of the topic I was required to submit my book to the DoD prepublication office for review and approval of the content. I did so in mid-July of 2015 and, after a 10-month review period, I received my book back with large parts of the content marked out. The editors at the publisher did an outstanding job working around the significant gaps in the text; however, the reader is likely to sense that something is missing, which is in fact the case. I ask the reader's forbearance and hope that they, like myself and CRC Press, agree that there is still a great deal of useful and unique information in my book.

LTC (Ret) William C. Buhrow
*"Biometrician"*
*Lorton, VA*

# ACKNOWLEDGMENTS

When one has a significant life accomplishment, thanking one's parents is appropriate. So in that regard, I do that here. My mother and father have certainly been supportive of my educational and professional pursuits, as well as being great parents—so, for that, I acknowledge their role in my success. In addition to thanking both of them for their great parentage, I want to particularly thank my father, Gary Buhrow, for his personal support for this project. Because he is both a smart and very articulate man and *not* a biometrics expert, I asked him to review my chapters from the layman's standpoint to make sure that my writing was both grammatically correct and cogent. He did this very well and I'm sure that both the readers and my editors have been well served by his efforts. I know I have.

I've known MG (Ret) John Custer since the days when he was Major Custer and I was Captain Buhrow in the 125th Military Intelligence Battalion at Schofield Barracks, Hawaii. He went on to an illustrious Army career, which included serving as the top intelligence officer (J2) of the U.S. Central Command throughout the initial years of the wars in Iraq and Afghanistan. Despite the huge differences in our professional lives in the years since we served together, we have stayed in touch and I count him as a friend in addition to being a former comrade. I could not have asked for a more appropriate person to write the Foreword for this book, and am grateful that he accepted my request to do so.

I also want to thank my former colleague and current friend, Allen Wight, for applying his extensive technical background and knowledge of biometrics to provide an honest assessment of the more technical portions of the book. After working side by side with Allen for a year while supporting DIA's Identity Intelligence Project Office, I came to (begrudgingly) appreciate his intelligence *and* his candor. Allen's comments and recommendations, most of which I accepted, made significant improvements to the text in a number of areas.

I'd also like to thank the few folks that I asked for interviews, particularly my friend and personal hero, Sean Falconi (see his vignette in Chapter 3); the former "Baroness of Biometrics" in Iraq, Colonel (Ret) Natalie Jacaruso; one of the original creators of the BAT system, Anthony Iasso; one of the early pioneers of military biometric operations, Jerry Jackson; and Vinnie Johns, who fielded the first biometric base-access systems in Iraq. These people had first-hand knowledge of some of the key developments in U.S. military biometrics and helped fill in the gaps in my personal biometrics experience.

The Author (r), Captain Sean Falconi (c) and Colonel José Smith (l) at Bagram Airbase, Afghanistan, in June 2009.

Finally, I'd like to thank my publisher Taylor & Francis Group, LLC, for agreeing to take on a topic that had never been written about before by someone who had never written a book before. I hope we both at least break even on this project; although for me it's not about the paycheck but about starting a more intelligent and holistic approach to the military use of biometrics. Of course, I likely would never have found my publisher were it not for my friend and former employer, Alex Anyse from MASY Group, who, when I told him of my interest in writing about biometrics, put me in touch with a former employee and author, Jenni Hesterman. It was she who helped me make my initial contact with Taylor & Francis, and I thank her for it.

# AUTHOR

**William C. Buhrow** was born and raised in Louisville, Kentucky. He attended Wake Forest University and graduated in 1983 with a BA in history and a commission as a Military Intelligence Officer in the United States Army. Bill served in a variety of overseas assignments and earned a master's in strategic intelligence from the Defense Intelligence College before leaving active service in 1993 for a position as a civilian intelligence analyst with the Defense Intelligence Agency. He returned to active service in 2003 with duty as an intelligence officer for the Army's Deputy Chief of Staff for Intelligence (G2). In 2007, he began a series of active duty tours with the U.S. Army's Biometrics Task Force/Biometrics Identity Management Agency, where he served in a variety of roles. He retired from the Army in 2012, and has since worked as a contractor supporting a number of DoD clients in the areas of biometrics and identity intelligence. Bill currently lives in northern Virginia.

# 1

# Why Do We Need Biometrics?

> Biometrics is a key capability that can identify the enemy, denying him the anonymity he needs to hide and strike at will. The ability to identify and verify individuals is also critical to ensure secure and expeditious business functions. As these biometrics capabilities are applied through various tactics, techniques and processes, they enable a wide range of possible missions, from military operations to business functions, that protect national interests.
>
> **Biometrics Identity Management Agency**
> **Annual Report FY10**

Mao Tse Tung wrote that "the guerrilla must move amongst the people as a fish swims in the sea." Today's insurgents, terrorists, and criminals seek to blend in with the people and become indistinguishable from them. Just as the local Viet Cong guerillas were often farmers by day and fighters by night, so have many of our enemies' leaders and fighters in recent conflicts in Iraq and Afghanistan hidden behind a mask of anonymity while staging attacks on the personnel and facilities of the United States and our allies. It is obviously critical that any force fighting an insurgency, battling terrorists, or facing an organized criminal threat will need a way to cull these bad actors from the general populace; but how?

There are many ways to distinguish friend from foe by establishing or verifying an individual's identity. If operating in a country with reliable and verifiable identity documents and mechanisms, the documentation can be presented by an unknown individual encountered in the battlespace and used by a friendly force to establish the individual's true identity.

## NOT A NEW CAPABILITY BUT NEW TO THE BATTLEFIELD

Biometrics in the form of fingerprints have been used for well over a hundred years as a way of ascertaining and confirming identity for law enforcement purposes. Through most of the 20th Century modern militaries have not had the same need to identify individuals on the battlefield because the focus was on identifying organizations (i.e., military units) and weapon systems like armored vehicles and aircraft. Furthermore, the enemy was normally in some sort of uniform and operating separately from the nonfighting populace, which made separating the two either fairly simple or even unnecessary. Where civilians did get in the way, they were either bypassed or became acceptable "collateral damage." When identifying individuals has been important, such as during the Vietnam War, U.S. forces tended to rely on information provided by intelligence sources, such as informants or human intelligence assets, or through interrogation of prisoners or other detainees. These efforts often suffered from the same weaknesses described previously and, in any event, were largely considered irrelevant to the kinds of "conventional" conflicts that the U.S. military and those of its allies prepared for during the Cold War era.

The end of the Cold War caused the U.S. and other militaries to begin focusing more on countering terrorism, low-intensity conflict, and military operations other than war, although not necessarily on counterinsurgency combat operations that tend to occur amongst a friendly or neutral populace and are directed against a nontraditional, nonuniformed foe. These kinds of operations face a number of challenges that are not present in the large-scale conventional conflicts the United States engaged in, and prepared for, in the Twentieth Century. First, the nature of the new threat places a premium on a military force's ability to detect and *identify individual enemy combatants* who often choose to remain undetected and anonymous among the surrounding populace. Second, the limited nature of these conflicts and the smaller sized, often widely dispersed, threat elements mean that precise and efficient targeting using limited forces and weapon systems is important. Lastly, and perhaps most important, these conflicts are fought in and amongst a noncombatant populace, and this situation has a very significant impact upon the way in which the United States and its allies conduct military operations. At the very least, heightened concerns over the humanitarian consequences of military operations in populated areas means that these operations must be conducted in a manner that limits the impact upon the people who are not the intended target. In modern counter-insurgency doctrine, however, the need to protect the populace is not just a humanitarian requirement but an operational imperative, because winning the active support of the people and separating them from the insurgents is often as important to the ultimate success of the mission as is targeting the enemy.* Biometrics and the related intelligence processes have proven to be critical in enabling the U.S. military's ability to conduct counterinsurgency operations by helping to focus combat operations on the real enemy and thus limiting the effect of those operations on the local populace.

Although there had been some limited employment of biometrics in Iraq almost from the start of the conflict, two key events occurred in 1994 that both underscored the critical need for biometrics and highlighted the significant impact that the use of biometric capabilities can have on the battlefield. On December 21, 2004, an Iraqi national wearing the uniform of an Iraqi policeman was able to gain entry to a major U.S. Forward Operating Base (FOB) on the outskirts of Mosul (see Figure 1.1).

**Figure 1.1** This photo shows the damage to a dining facility on the coalition base in Mosul caused by a suicide bomber. The attacker was an Iraqi who used a stolen Iraqi police uniform and forged ID to gain access to the base and it spurred the search for more reliable ways to screen individuals entering U.S. and coalition facilities.

* Former French Army Officer David Galula developed a theory of counterinsurgency based upon his experience in the Algerian War that focused squarely on the importance of the civilian populace and in separating them from the insurgents.

Apparently allowed entrance based upon his stolen uniform and forged ID card, he made his way to the base dining facility, where he detonated the suicide vest he was wearing under his bulky policeman's coat. The resultant blast blew a huge hole in the roof of the facility and killed 14 U.S. soldiers, four U.S. civilian contractors, and four Iraqi soldiers. The ease with which this individual gained access to a major U.S./Coalition military base led to an immediate effort to implement new force-protection capabilities, which included biometrics. Eventually, access to all U.S. and Coalition bases throughout Iraq, Southwest Asia and, finally, Afghanistan would be protected by biometrics screening and badging systems, most notably the Biometrics Identification System for Access (BISA). These systems proved their worth by preventing a repeat of similar attacks such as that at Mosul.

Also in 2004, two major military operations occurred to eliminate the insurgents' use of the town of Fallujah in the western Al Anbar Province as a base for operations. The First Battle of Fallujah took place following the seizure and gruesome murder in early April of three Blackwater contractors who happened to stray into the town by mistake. The picture (Figure 1.2) of their bodies handing from a bridge into the town proved to be one of the seminal images of the war and served as the catalyst for a coalition operation aimed at eliminating the insurgency in the area. Although the initial operation, which began on April 4, succeeded in suppressing the local insurgents, the Coalition's inability to secure the city and to prevent the reemergence of the insurgents and terrorists led to another Coalition attack that began on November 7 of that year.

The Second Battle of Fallujah was also successful in disrupting the Fallujah insurgency; however, it was the follow-on phases of the operation that finally eliminated the city as a base for enemy activities. After the previous attack, the security of the town was turned over to a hastily assembled and highly suspect Iraqi force. This time, the United States and its allies were determined to retain control over the hard-won territory to prevent a reemergence of the insurgency. They accomplished this by surrounding the city with a berm and barbed wire enclosure that prevented access except through a few tightly controlled entry and exit points. In addition, the entire population was removed from the city and only allowed back after military operations ceased and all military-aged Iraqi male (MAM) residents were biometrically enrolled and issued biometrically enabled ID cards. From then on, all MAMs reentering the city were screened with a biometric system to ensure that they were truly part of the

**Figure 1.2** This 2004 photo of the aftermath the brutal killing of three U.S. contractors in Fallujah, Iraq became one of the most iconic of the early Iraq war. The incident led to two major battles to wrest control of the city from insurgents, the second of which featured the first successful widespread use of biometrics in a military operation.

local populace and not outsiders trying to infiltrate the town. In addition, roving patrols and check-points were used throughout the city to check the identities of MAMs and to verify those identities against the ID cards they were carrying. This effort, coupled with the eventual emergence of a local Iraqi anti-insurgent movement (aka the Sons of Liberty) succeeded in eliminating Fallujah as an insurgent and terrorist base. Similar efforts were undertaken elsewhere in the majority Sunni Anbar Province, which, for a period, transformed the formerly restive area into something of a model of stability.

Despite the significant challenges to maximizing the employment of biometrics by military forces, it appears that there will continue to be a need for military biometrics and identity operations following the withdrawal of the U.S. and its allies from active combat operations in Afghanistan. Barring any major change to U.S. defense policy, we will continue to deploy forces around the world in bases (temporary or semi-permanent) that need protecting. There will continue to be terrorists that we will need to pursue and capture or kill. And, there will continue to be a need to positively identify the members of military foreign and security forces with whom we interact. Therefore, there will continue to be a need to properly employ the capabilities that exist today to identify and verify the identities of individuals in support of a wide range of military and supporting operations—it is to this need that I turn to in the rest of this book.

# 2

# Biometrics Basics

In the last chapter, I discussed the reason why biometrics is a critical enabler to military operations. Assuming that the reader has accepted that proposition and is still with me, I'll move on in this chapter with an overview of some the basic concepts that underlie the use of biometrics on the battlefield, such as the difference between "identification" and "verification" using biometrics, the broad mission types that biometrics can support, biometrics modalities and matching, the relationships between biometrics and forensics, and biometrics and intelligence, and data sharing and communications. My intent is to provide enough detail on these issues to support the rest of the book, not to make the reader a biometrics expert. More in-depth information on many of the topics is included in the appendices.

Chapter 2 will address the following key concepts:

- There are important differences between identification and verification and all "identifications" are not the same.
- There are many different ways to collect biometrics and all can be used to support a military operation.
- Modalities matter: use the right ones for the mission and the environment.
- A "match" is not a sure thing, but it can be very close.
- Forensics is a means of biometrics collection (aka "latent biometrics").
- There is a symbiotic relationship between biometrics and intelligence.

- Data sharing is crucial: across organizations, nations, and applications.
- Good communications are critical for effective biometrics operations.
- Biometrics has many uses: offense, defense (i.e., force protection), intelligence, and supporting activities (e.g., medical, resource control/management, border control).

## WHAT IS BIOMETRICS?

The Department of Defense Biometrics Glossary defines biometrics as both a characteristic and a process. As a characteristic, it refers to a biological or behavioral feature of an individual (such as the iris, fingerprint, or voice pattern) that can be measured and used for automated recognition. As a process, it refers to the automated means of measuring and comparing these features, in order to establish the identity of an individual.* To that official definition, I would also add that biometrics refers to a set of technologies used in the identification process. The term "automated" is important, since we all perform identification tasks frequently throughout the day, when we meet someone new or come in contact with someone we have already met. Confirming someone's identity visually is not considered a biometric activity, nor is the manual comparison of photographs and fingerprints that law enforcement agencies have been doing for a hundred years. Despite this distinction, we'll see later that even with our "automated" capabilities, there is still a significant manual effort that goes into making biometrics work in a military setting.

## IDENTIFICATION VS. VERIFICATION

Biometrics are generally described as having two broad types of use. The first, and the one on which we will primarily focus in this book, is the use of biometrics to "identify" an unknown person. Such a use involves collecting biometrics from someone we are encountering and whose identity is unknown to us. This could be an individual at a checkpoint or during an operation, or it could be a person who is applying for a job on

* Biometrics Identity Management Agency, Biometrics Glossary Version 6.0, April 2012. Portions are included in Appendix E.

our overseas facility. In most cases, that person will at least provide us a name which may or may not be correct, and they may also have some documents that validate their identity—although it could also be someone we've detained after an attack, who may not give us a name at all (or certainly *not* the right one).* In order to determine who this person really is, we will collect their biometrics, along with other data, and use them to determine if we have the same person in our database by comparing the newly collected biometrics to all those we have previously collected. The result of this One-to-Many (aka 1:N) comparison is called "identification." Identification seeks to establish a unique or distinct identity for an individual, but that doesn't mean it is necessarily an accurate or true identity (more on that below).

Identification allows us to both determine if an unknown individual we have encountered has a previously established identity in our database(s) and if that identity has derogatory information (e.g., suspected criminal activity or militant activity or job termination) associated with it. In many cases, as noted above, this individual will identify himself by an alias in order to hide both this previously established identity, and the negative information attached to it. Using biometrics, we can tie this individual to his previous, alternative identities, which can allow us to make more informed decisions about questions regarding detention or release, hiring, or training. Identification can be a lengthy process, dependent upon the size of the database we are using, and the type of biometrics we are working with. Matching fingerprints from a suspected IED (improvised explosive device) emplacer against latent fingerprints collected from an attack scene could take hours or longer due to the need for human interaction in the matching process, the often low quality of the forensically collected fingerprints, and the size of the database.

Verification typically occurs after an individual has been biometrically enrolled into a database and his or her identity recorded within the system.† On subsequent biometric encounters (such as with a biometric door lock to a secure facility), the individual presents some means of non-biometric identification, such as a smart card or pin number (or even just

* Another scenario is to collect latent fingerprints from an attack site, suspected terrorist safe-house, or from captured enemy equipment; or we could collect biometrics off an insurgent killed in action. In these cases, no identity will obviously be claimed, although information might be found that provide some indication of a possible identity.

† These kinds of biometric collections are normally voluntary and performed to register a person for possible employment, allow them to access a facility, or for the provision of some kind of resource or service.

a name), that allows the biometric file associated with the individual to be pulled from the database and compared to a new biometric collection from that individual (also known as a One-to-One or 1:1 comparison). If the two sets of biometrics match, the individual's identity is verified. Because the comparison is a single biometric file to another and is normally performed using a single, local database, the verification process is typically much faster than identification.

One note of caution is in order here is how and when we use terms like "identity" and "identification." In biometrics, the term "identification" is often a bit of a misnomer because in many cases all we can do (and perhaps all we need to do) is to establish a consistent identity for an individual, not necessarily the true one. For example, a suspected insurgent may have been initially enrolled into a biometric database with a false name and false biographic information. If that same individual is encountered again and his biometrics collected and matched against our previously collected data, he would be "identified" as having the same false identity he provided before. That's not necessarily a bad thing, since often "locking down" an individual to a single identity can be sufficient to track him or her across time and space and to link the individual to activities or events (such as insurgent attacks or crimes) with which he or she would prefer not to be associated. In this case, it may not really matter what the individual's actual name is as long as we have enough information to make an informed decision about what to do with the person (such as whether or not to detain, hire, or train him or her). Likewise, if I am using biometrics simply to verify that the person I previously "identified" and hired for a job on my base (say, "John") is the same person who is coming to work every day and not some criminal or terrorist posing as him, then the individual's true identity may be immaterial. All I need to know is that I hired John to work on my base and it really is John who I allow to access my facility every day.

Obviously, determining an individual's true identity *is* important in many cases, such as when we are doing intelligence or investigative work to build a case against a criminal suspect, or in order to target a suspected terrorist. It can also be important if we are vetting someone for access to a critical/sensitive facility or hiring them as a member of an armed security force. In such cases, it's not sufficient to simply identify or verify them against data in our biometrics system; we need to perform a much deeper analysis using criminal investigative or analytical techniques and tools to discover if there is other nonbiometrics information that can lead us to an understanding of the "true" identity of this individual and a deeper knowledge of his activities and associates. In biometrics intelligence, such a full picture of an individual may be aggregated and stored in a database as the individual's "digital dossier". The data stored here can be used to determine if the individual should be added to a watch list or targeted for an operation to kill or capture. In these kinds of situations, the role of biometrics is to provide additional data to the investigative or intelligence effort and to provide the way to definitely link that individual to this data if he or she is encountered in the battlespace.

## ACQUIRING BIOMETRIC DATA

There are many different ways that biometrics can be collected in order to populate a military database. Perhaps the most recognized means of acquiring biometrics is the *direct or live collection* of biometrics from a subject. These collections are often performed in the context of an enrollment, during which, both biometrics and associated textual data about the subject and the circumstances of the collection are recorded. Such collections will occur throughout a military operation by forces on patrol, at the scenes of attacks, as part of a detention process, at a facility access point, and many others. These collections are also normally performed using automated biometric collection systems. The systems collect the data and format it digitally, allow the data to be compared to previous collections stored on the device, and enable transmission to a remote database for matching against a much larger dataset, for long-term storage, and, potentially, for sharing with others.

Direct collections can also be performed the old-fashioned way, using manual mechanisms such as ink and fingerprints cards (Figure 2.1). Even when a force has access to biometric collection systems, it may still want to use hard-copy fingerprint collection, under certain circumstances. For instance, when I was in Afghanistan, we visited a counter-IED unit whose leadership suggested that the use of ink and card fingerprint collection might expand their collection efforts by providing a collection capability to many more soldiers beyond those currently equipped and trained to use the automated systems. Facial photos can also be collected without using a biometric collection device.* The challenge for these kinds of col-

* Given the fact that many soldiers and marines carry their cellphones with them, this is a collection methodology that needs to be exploited, perhaps with the development of a simple app to provide some consistent formatting to the collection and recording of data.

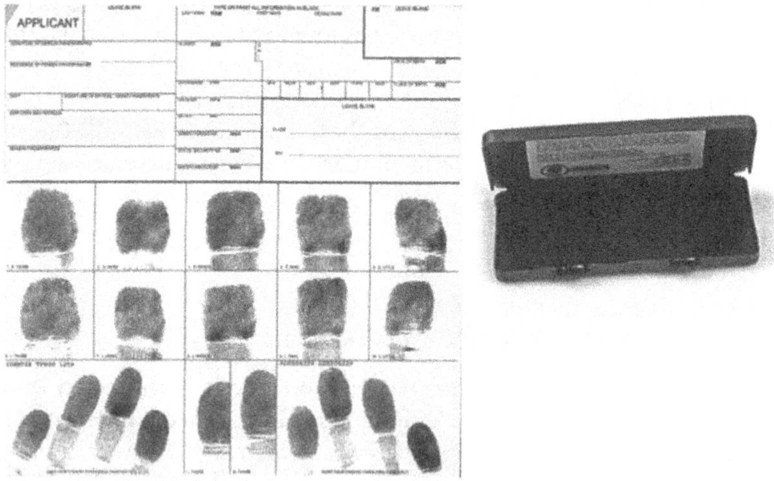


**Figure 2.1** Collecting biometrics the old-fashioned way, with ink pad and card, is still a viable alternative in some situations.

lections is that there will not be any immediate feedback on the quality of the collection, nor on whether the collection matches any previously collected data. In fact, no match will occur at all until the data are turned into a properly formatted digital file and ingested into a biometric database. There is also a need to provide the means to collect and associate the critical textual data that should accompany the biometric data.

The last of the direct collection methods I want to highlight is the collection of biometric data using forensic techniques. I will not go into great detail here, since I cover the issue below, but it is important to know that the U.S. military developed processes and provided equipment and training to allow the common frontline soldier to perform what became known as "Tactical Site Exploitation" or TSE.* TSE was designed so that evidence could be collected by troops on the ground, at sites of attacks, or

* TSE is related to, but distinct from, a similar but much more sophisticated process called "Sensitive Site Exploitation" (SSE). SSE was normally performed at locations of greater operational or even strategic interest, such as high-level terrorist safe-houses or suspected chemical/biological warfare facilities. SSE is also typically performed by more highly and technically trained personnel using more technically sophisticated equipment and is often the purview of special operations forces.

locations where enemy equipment and documents were discovered.* With a fairly limited amount of training and relatively simple collection and storage kits, soldiers could collect and preserve latent fingerprints, chemical residue, and perhaps DNA for subsequent exploitation and analysis by forensics experts and intelligence analysts. Such data could be subsequently used for identification purposes, intelligence analysis, or even to support legal action.

Beyond the kinds of direct biometric collections described above, there are many ways that data, even vast quantities of data, *can be acquired indirectly*. I like to refer to these as the "Beg, Buy, Steal" methods of biometric collection. By the "Beg" part, I am referring to the development of *biometric data-sharing arrangements* between friendly or allied countries that facilitate the transfer of biometric data among them. As I will discuss later in the book, these kinds of arrangements can be very complicated to develop and to put into operation, even between the closest allies, due to differing legal and regulatory policies, system and data incompatibility, and the absence of technical and operational processes needed to identify the data to be shared and to actually share it. Still, when successfully implemented, these arrangements provide the type and quantity of data to a military force that would take months of direct collection operations to produce.†

There are vast quantities of identity data held by commercial data aggregators and data brokers that might be available for purchase, much as commercial retailers frequently purchase such data. While the biometric component of these datasets is likely to be limited to facial photos, such data, if present at all, could certainly be useful for intelligence analysis or even to support an advanced matching system (see "Afterword," Chapter 9). Another variant of this method would be to trade for it, perhaps by building a biometric capability for another country, contingent upon receiving a share of the collected data. There are many countries that lack the resources to develop or purchase biometric systems on their own, but who would be willing to share some of their collected data in exchange

* Prior to the development of site exploitation, soldiers raiding an insurgent facility would typically leave vast amounts of exploitable information behind after they kicked in the door and killed or captured the inhabitants.

† Any force planning potential or upcoming military operations should identify who else may have data on the country or region in which it is going to be operating. Because of the technical and, oftentimes, political complications, data-sharing arrangements must be developed as early in the planning process as possible, even if their implementation is contingent upon future conditions.

for being provided the resources to collect it. This arrangement might be more politically palatable for a country that agrees to share biometrics collected from other than their own citizens, such as immigration data, or data they collect during the kind of coalition-based military operations such as those conducted in Iraq and Afghanistan.

## WHAT ARE MODALITIES?

I previously defined biometrics as being about the "measurable characteristics" of a person. These characteristics are known as "modalities," and the number of modalities being studied and evaluated for their potential use in biometric identification and verification is growing. The most commonly used and referenced modality is fingerprints, which have been widely used in the U.S. criminal justice system beginning with the New York State Prison system in 1903.* As any student of criminal justice or fan of the "CSI" or "Law and Order" shows will also know, DNA evidence is often the critical element in many criminal investigations, but it is also a modality that can be used to identify deceased suicide bombers. The use of face images to identify individuals (i.e., facial recognition) is becoming of great interest within the military, intelligence, and security communities due to its ability to be collected covertly and from a distance. In addition to these more commonly known and employed modalities, there has been research into more esoteric means of identification, such as ear-lobe shape, body odor, gait, and others. Essentially, almost any aspect of an individual's body, behavior, or actions that may be unique to the individual has, or will be, the target of some research to assess its utility as a means of identification.

Each modality has certain aspects that may distinguish it from another, and these distinguishing aspects can help a user determine which kind of modality to use in a particular military setting. Military users should always consider these particularly important modality factors when planning for biometric operations.

- Collectability: How easy is it to collect this modality?
- Acceptability: Are their cultural issues that will negatively impact on collection?
- Uniqueness: How unique is it to a single individual?

* National Science and Technology Council, Biometrics History, August 7, 2006, pages 3, 7.

- Universality: How common is this modality in a particular population?
- Accuracy: How accurate is this modality in matching, using the database(s) we have access to?

A more complete list and a chart comparing these factors across the most common modalities are contained in Appendix B. But the real importance of these factors for our purposes—which I will address in more detail in the next chapter—is how they impact the use of that modality in a particular operation. At this point, it's just important to know that there are operational considerations that can and should influence which modalities to collect during a given operation and in a given operational environment. In other words, "modalities matter."

## BIOMETRIC MATCHING: WHAT DOES IT REALLY MEAN?

After a military user has selected the modality he or she wants to use and has collected data this during a biometric-supported mission, what happens next? The whole point of biometric collection is to compare the newly collected biometric sample against a set of samples collected previously to determine if any are the same. The process is called "biometric matching" and can be performed immediately at the time of biometric capture, based upon data stored on the collecting device itself.* Since collection devices have a limited storage capacity, biometric collections are also normally transmitted to a separate database, which could be located in the local area or region, or be thousands of miles away. The results of the comparison between the newly collected data and data previously collected and stored in the remote database are transmitted back to the collecting unit in a manner determined by available communications means. Even if this process does not result in a match, the newly collected data will normally be stored in the remote database (or at least on the collection device) to be compared to future collections.

Typically, an operator using a biometric collection device will receive some notification that the sample just collected matched against another sample. But what does that really mean? Well, what it doesn't mean is

* Most biometric collection devices are capable of storing a certain number of collected biometric files against which new collections can be compared for immediate matching. Most systems are also able to upload files collected elsewhere, such as those files contained in a watchlist of individuals assessed to be "Persons of Interest."

that there is a 100% mathematical certainty that the two samples are from the same person. In fact, the result of the matching process, whether it occurs on the collection device itself or at a central database, is not a 100% sure thing, but, rather, a mathematical probability. Even a match that results from the comparison of DNA samples, considered the most accurate modality, is not a mathematical certainty (although it is pretty close).* Likewise, a result that indicates there is no match from the comparison of my newly collected biometric to biometrics samples in existing database(s) is also not a mathematical certainty. There are many technical and operational factors that can have a major impact upon the accuracy of the matching process, and these will be discussed later. For the military user, the important thing to know is that the process is not infallible even under the best conditions, with the best equipment, and using well-trained operators. So, be careful how you use the results of this matching process and realize that a holistic solution to combat identification, which takes multiple datasets into account, is always better than relying on biometrics alone, however powerful they may be.

## BIOMETRICS AND FORENSICS

During the kinds of military operations that the United States and its allies have engaged in over the past decade, some of the most valuable biometrics collections have occurred not from direct encounters between a Coalition soldier with a biometrics device and an unknown Iraqi or Afghan, but those biometric samples that have been taken off of captured enemy materials or documents. The reason for this should be rather obvious—most of the routine biometrics collections made across the operational area are either for fairly innocuous reasons, such as access control at a base gate or random collections in the battlespace. On the other hand, if I collect a fingerprint off of an IED component, I can be pretty sure that any match that results (with the above caution in mind) is pointing me to a bad guy or one of his supporters.

Unfortunately, I have observed that within the military biometrics community, there has been some confusion between those who practice biometrics as a discipline, and those who perform forensic analysis. Part

* A 2010 RAND Study on the DoD use of DNA described one of its advantages as being that "everyone's DNA is different," which is a common misconception. In fact, maternal/identical twins (or identical triplets, quadruplets, etc.) share the same DNA code.

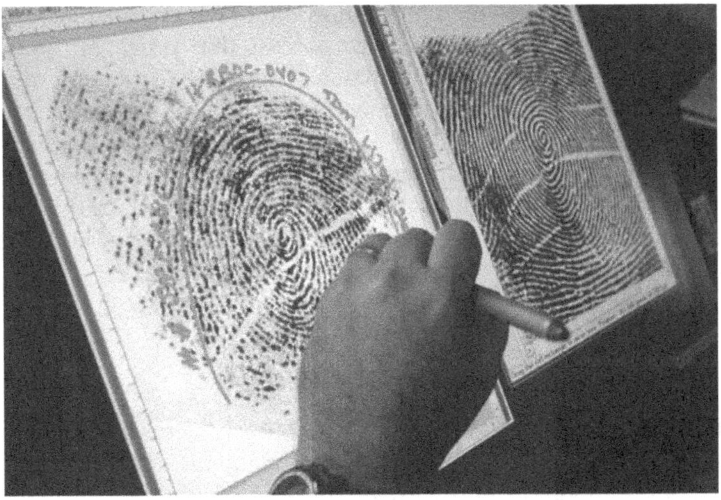

**Figure 2.2** The collection, processing, and matching of latent biometrics plays a critical role in any military biometrics operation. (Adapted from http://www.army.mil/article/71071/.)

of the problem is in the terminology. Forensics is a discreet and well-established discipline practiced by law enforcement, security (including digital/computer forensics), and intelligence personnel AND it is a method of obtaining biometric samples for processing and matching as part of the biometric identification process. My former colleague, Allen Wight, uses the term "latent biometrics" to refer to the biometrics collected from crime scenes or locations of attacks, enemy equipment for documents, or from clandestine collection activities. While this terminology would be a good way to relieve some of the forensics–biometrics conflict, by helping to distinguish forensics in the law-enforcement process from forensics in the biometric-collection activity, it is unfortunately not widely used, at least within the military or intelligence realms. So we'll just say that in regards to the biometric process, forensics is a collection technique used to extract biometrics samples that were left in the past (Figure 2.2).

## BIOMETRICS AND INTELLIGENCE

If I were to sum up the symbiotic relationship that exists between biometrics and intelligence, I would say that: "biometrics needs intelligence to be meaningful, while intelligence needs biometrics to be actionable." Put another way, it is the intelligence process that provides the critical information that indicates why the match is important and helps us determine what to do about it. Without this information, all we would know is that unidentified Subject A is the same person as unidentified Subject B. Even if we had collected a name and some biographic data from both, we probably would not know that newly identified Subject A/B is also an insurgent financier whose activities have been detailed in both Signals and Human Intelligence reporting.

## DATA SHARING

The ability to share data rapidly and seamlessly across an operational network, between operational biometrics elements and strategic systems, among national-level organizations, and across national boundaries is crucial to the success of any large-scale biometrics effort. However, there are often significant technical, operational/procedural, and legal/policy issues that must be addressed in order to ensure that the right data gets where it needs to go, in an operationally relevant timeframe.* Despite the complexities of data sharing, there are technical solutions that can ameliorate at least some of the difficulties of moving data across systems that employ different database structures and differing data formats. Therefore, when planning for a military operation, it is important to understand the biometrics capabilities and related policies and processes of all friendly operational elements (including potential coalition members), and to incorporate that knowledge into our biometrics planning.

* As it often turns out, while technical issues such as the compatibility of systems and data formats can often require substantial efforts from big-brained engineers and data experts, it is often legal and policy concerns that prove the biggest stumbling blocks to the development of effective biometrics data-sharing capabilities. For example, sharing biometrics data between intelligence and law enforcement elements often gives lawyers fits, while sharing the biometrics data and associated analysis across national boundaries may run afoul of national privacy policies or existing bilateral or multinational agreements. The development of new policies and agreements to facilitate data sharing during an upcoming military operation needs to begin *before* the bullets start to fly.

# 3

# General Operational Issues

In the first two chapters, I outlined some of the basic concepts that show how biometrics work and the key contributions that biometrics can make to various kinds of military missions. My intent with these chapters was to provide just enough detail to prepare the reader for a more in-depth discussion of how a military force can prepare itself to execute the various military biometrics missions I will discuss throughout the book, without getting bogged down in too much technical minutiae. There is much more on the technical aspects of biometrics in the appendices, particularly in Appendices B and C.

In this chapter, I am going to address the following key concepts:

- Biometrics operations must be well-planned and prepared for in advance, to include the following issues:
  - Data type and quantity
    - Identifying biometrics data requirements
    - Developing a Biometrics Collection Plan
    - Beginning to build the database *before* the operation
  - Collection systems
    - Choosing the right system for the mission or maximizing the effectiveness of the systems you have
  - Matching schemes: on system, with BEWL, remote database
  - Databases: forward, remote, multinational
  - Communications and data movement
  - Effective policies

    - TTPs (Tactics, Techniques, and Procedures) and training
- Collection considerations
    - Maximizing collection opportunities
    - Collecting the highest quality and most complete set of biometrics possible
- Modalities matter: the modality must match the mission
- Plan for multinational operations

## ADVANCED PREPARATION IS KEY

The U.S. military places a great effort on being prepared for the next conflict in order to ensure that we have the organizations, training, equipment, and doctrine in place, so that our forces are ready for the first battle. War plans are normally created well in advance of any anticipated operation, units are trained to conduct the kinds of missions that they are expected to undertake, soldiers are properly equipped, and all manner of logistical resources are identified and positioned as close to the operational theater as possible. Unfortunately, in the case of biometrics, almost none of the normal elements of combat readiness had been established prior to beginning operations in Afghanistan or, later, in Iraq. There were no biometrics organizations established; there was little, if any, operational equipment beyond a few prototypes; and there were certainly no operational policies, procedures, or training. Now that the war in Iraq is over and operations in Afghanistan are winding down, we must ensure that we are better prepared to maximize our biometrics support to military operations at the start of our next conflict and to do so across the spectrum of military missions.

At the start of any military operation, it is likely that our biometrics enrollments will produce few matches. This was certainly the case in Iraq and Afghanistan. Because we began those operations without establishing a supporting biometrics database, data collected by military personnel during operations produced few direct results, other than populating our database, for the simple reason that there was little existing data against which to match our new collections. In such a scenario, it may take considerable time before we reach the level of data collection from which we begin to see significant results. In Iraq and Afghanistan, this point became known as the "tipping" point, and it took years of biometrics collection to reach that milestone.

## SELECTING THE RIGHT SYSTEM FOR THE OPERATION (OR MODIFYING THE WRONG ONE)

Collection systems employed in any military biometrics effort should reflect the kinds of data we intend to collect, the missions that biometrics will support, and the operational environment. Is the mission primarily defensive in nature and/or will it involve extensive combat operations? Will combat operations be conducted by forces operating out of static facilities or by small units disconnected from fixed infrastructure? Will there be large bases that need protecting? Will we hire members of the local populace to work on our facilities? Will we run a detention system? Will biometrics collections be performed by uniformed personnel in the field, contractors at fixed facilities, or both? These are just some of the questions that need to be addressed during operations planning to help ensure we deploy with the right biometrics tools for our mission.

Most militaries make at least some effort to ensure that they procure military systems based upon an analysis of future threats and future technical developments. However, as we have seen with biometrics, it is not always possible to foresee the need for new kinds of operations and new kinds of technology needed to conduct them. Even a successful planning effort may fail to anticipate new methods of employing a system or the new technical developments that may make additional capabilities available during the course of a military mission. Fortunately, in the case of biometrics, systems were often initially designed and, in some cases, modified fairly rapidly through relatively small-scale government-run advanced/rapid technology projects or by commercial vendors. However, once these systems came under the direction of the formal acquisition/development process, our ability to keep up with the nearly continuous changes to operational requirements proved to be a major challenge.*

The U.S. military began operations in Iraq and Afghanistan using biometrics collection systems that were not optimal for these environments, particularly in the case of Afghanistan. The Biometrics Automated Toolset or BAT and the Handheld Interagency Identity Detection Equipment (HIIDE) were the predominant tactical collection systems at the start of combat operations. They were adequate for the

* More on that in Chapter 8 (Conclusion).

collection of biometrics and associated biographic and contextual data in an environment with a relatively well-developed infrastructure, such as in Iraq, but they were less well-suited for the operational environment in Afghanistan, where communication networks were much less robust and where many operations were conducted at isolated and dispersed locations. The negative impact of the Afghan operational environment on the BAT/HIIDE system was considerable and resulted in a serious degradation in the effectiveness of biometric operations in the country.

Another problem with the BAT system was that it was not really designed to be operated in a field environment. For example, even though the system and all its accessories were originally packaged and delivered to units in camouflage backpacks, all of the components were separate and it was a fairly lengthy process to assemble everything and prepare the system for operation. Moreover, while the main component of the BAT is a ruggedized Toughbook Laptop, the rest of the components were basically commercial off the shelf (COTS) products, such as digital cameras and iris and fingerprint capture devices, which were definitely not designed to be soldier-, marine- or Afghanistan-proof. Finally, because the system was designed around a basic commercial laptop, it required commercial power, which restricted its use in many operational scenarios, particularly in Afghanistan.*

Fortunately, smart soldiers and contract support personnel working for ISAF's Task Force Biometrics at Bagram Airbase were able to devise ways to overcome at least some of the system's shortcomings. Most notably, they devised a way to repackage the BAT into a much more mobile and tactically useful system by preconnecting all the components and carefully packing the complete system into a Pelican carrying case (Figure 3.1). Equally important, if not more so, they devised a method to run the system off military power by grafting on a military power cable, which would allow the system to plug into any standard military power source.† These ingenious modifications would allow a unit to take the BAT into the field and quickly set it up to begin operating within minutes. The

* See Appendix C for a more complete description of the BAT/HIIDE and other common biometrics systems.

† Electric power could be provided by a generator or by tactical vehicles such as an armored High-Mobility, Multi-Wheeled Vehicle (HMMWV), which has external power ports to which power cables with the proper connectors can be attached.

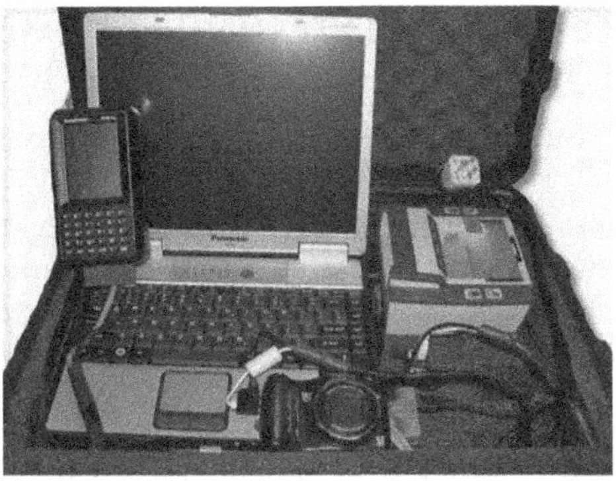

**Figure 3.1** Members of Task Force Biometrics developed and assembled Mobile BAT Kits at Bagram Airbase, Afghanistan.

initial kits were produced in an assembly line fashion by personnel at the TF (Task Force) Biometrics HQ and became so popular with ISAF units that they no longer wanted the standard issue BAT kits. Attempts to get the Army's acquisition/development system to produce these kits proved unsuccessful, likely because the modifications were beyond the scope of the current contract under which the BATs were acquired. Although the Task Force continued to produce small quantities of the popular system by hand on site, they could never meet the demand from the units in the field.

So the lesson regarding biometrics systems is that planning before an operation will help ensure that units deploy with systems that are able to support the kinds of biometrics missions that will be performed and be able to operate effectively in the operational environment. However, it is likely that military units will continue to employ biometrics systems that require rapid modifications in order to maximize their capabilities, particularly in missions of longer duration. A rapid acquisition process, such as that provided by the Army's Rapid Equipping Force (REF) coupled with a forward support presence that includes representatives from the formal acquisition organizations (i.e., program management offices), will also be necessary so that biometrics devices can be quickly modified to react to changes in mission or methods of employment, and the identification of system shortcomings, and to keep pace with rapid and continuous technical developments.

## MATCH YOUR MATCHING SCHEME TO THE MISSION AND THE SYSTEM

Most biometrics systems are capable of producing matches by comparing newly collected biometrics data to data previously collected by that device or by matching against data contained in a watchlist that has been uploaded to the device. Most are also able to transmit collected data to an external/remote database.* In this case, the match is performed at the database, and the results are reported back to the submitter (hopefully in an operationally relevant timeframe).

Ideally, a military force would want the ability to use all three matching methods, but that may not be feasible because of collection device capabilities, the operational environment, available communications, or other factors (see Table 3.1). All systems possess the capability to immediately match against data held within the system itself, which could be data collected previously on the particular device, or it could be using data collected elsewhere and uploaded to the device. Such a "match on device" matching scheme limits that size of the database against which newly collected data can be matched (and thus lessens the chances for achieving a match); however, this may be sufficient for some mission applications, such as when controlling access to humanitarian aid or verifying the identities of small numbers of foreign or host nation workers who need recurring access to a military installation. It is important to consider the data storage capabilities of the biometrics device being used as that can vary widely. The standard HIIDE, for example, can hold approximately 10,000 complete enrollment files, while a BAT can hold many times that number. If the mission involves using a single biometrics device, or set of devices, to identify individuals whose biometrics have not been previously collected by our systems, then matching only against the data stored on our devices is obviously not going to be of great value.

In particular, a match against an individual on the watchlist tends to have a higher degree of significance than other kinds of matches. However, it can take a significant amount of time to upload watchlist changes, dependent upon the type of system and the available communications

* Some of the newer devices have built-in communications capabilities, but most will have to interface with some kind of external communications system, such as a tactical military radio, cellular system, or satellite communications system. The BAT generally transmits and receives data by plugging into a network (unclassified or classified), while the HIIDE must link to a BAT to download collections and upload watchlist updates. More on the devices themselves can be found in Appendix D.

**Table 3.1** Comparison of Matching Schemes

| Matching Scheme | Description | Advantages | Disadvantages | Remarks |
|---|---|---|---|---|
| Match on system | Match only against files collected by the individual device or uploaded from other devices | • Communications is not a concern<br>• Immediate match results are provided | • Limited dataset to match against | • May be sufficient for certain operations or operational environments |
| Match against a watchlist | Match against dataset of watchlisted individuals | • Immediate match results provided<br>• Matches indicate POIs<br>• Communications not required during matching process<br>• Match results may include operational guidance | • Requires dedicated analytical effort to produce/update watchlist<br>• Communications required to receive watchlist updates | • Critical for timely tactical identification<br>• Can be used in conjunction with other matching schemes |
| Match against remote database | Matches produced after collections are transmitted from collecting device to a separate database | • Potentially large dataset maximizes chances for a match | • Requires reliable and near real-time communications between collector and database | • Database can be of varying sizes and composition |

connectivity, and some handheld or disconnected systems have gone for months without uploading watchlist updates. In such instances, once the watchlist updates were finally uploaded, matches have occurred against biometric collections that were done weeks or even months in the past.*

The final matching arrangement is to transmit new biometric collections to a remote database/matching system similar to the DoD Automated Biometric Identification System (ABIS). The advantage of such a process is that new collections are matched against the widest possible dataset, which can include data collected in another operational area or even in another part of the world. The challenge with such a matching scheme is that it is highly dependent upon the provision of reliable and capable communications links between the collector and the external database. For these reasons, if a remote database is to be used and communications connectivity is at all a concern, the process should be augmented by a watchlist that is continuously updated and transmitted to the collecting organizations for uploading on their biometric devices.

## THE DATABASE(S)

In a perfect world, the overall nature of the military mission, the kinds of biometrics operations being planned to support that mission, the operational environment, and the available communications infrastructure would all dictate the kind of database that will need to be established, and where that database will be located. However, we do not live in a perfect world, and to turn a phrase by former Secretary of Defense Donald Rumsfeld: "You don't go to war with the Biometrics Enterprise you want, you go to war with the Biometrics Enterprise you have."

Over time, communications shortfalls, data latency, and other operational considerations, spurred the call for the development of a regional biometrics database that could be located in or closer to the theater of operations and which would presumably be more responsive to combat elements. Development of a local database was not supported by the leadership of the Biometrics Identity Management Agency (BIMA) for a number of reasons. Eventually, continuous demands from the U.S.

* Not all operations or units will have the kind of dedicated intelligence support needed to create and update a BEWL, although it is possible for a local commander to create his own, less extensive or sophisticated version for his unit to use.

Central Command led to the emplacement of a forward server in the theater as part of a technology demonstration known as the "Last Tactical Mile" (which will be discussed more below). However, when I departed the BIMA in June 2012, the experiment had not been much of a success. Despite this experience, work continues on ways to make more data readily available to support the immediate needs of deployed forces, which, I think, deserves careful study.*

One variation of the forward database concept is to create a temporary database for military operations involving large numbers of foreign military forces. I will discuss this more later in this chapter, but I'll just say here that this issue, like the LTM (last tactical mile) concern I discussed earlier, deserves more study and consideration as a key capability of our future DoD Biometrics Enterprise.

## COMMUNICATIONS AND DATA MOVEMENT ARE CRITICAL

I've already described the critical nature of the communications links within the biometrics network and between biometrics and operational or intelligence elements, and this issue cannot be overstated (see chart below from GAO, showing biometrics data transmission times between October 2009 and October 2011). I will not readdress the communications problems associated with the data replication mechanism of the BAT system other than to say that problems identified with this system previously in Iraq were magnified in Afghanistan's poorer infrastructure, more challenging terrain, and more decentralized and remote operational scheme.

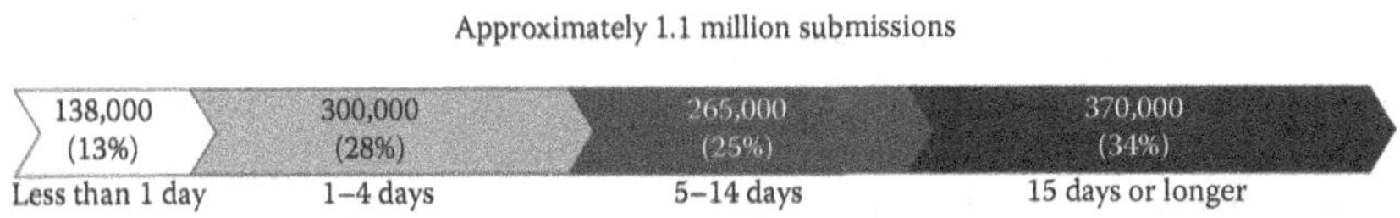

Source: GAO analysis of DOD data.

* Over the years of my time with BTF/BIMA, there were discussions about developing regionally focused datasets or even a regional or country-focused BEWL, but apparently the DoD biometric database was not configured to allow a subset of the data to be extracted. Such a feature would be a very valuable part of any future military biometrics database as it could allow a force to deploy for an operation with enough data to facilitate more immediate, time-sensitive matching, particularly in an environment where reliable communications connectivity to the central data set is not always available.

### THE MYTH OF FRAGO 41

Shortly after I arrived in Afghanistan, I began hearing about a Regional Command East (RC East) policy (known as "FRAGO 41) that supposedly prevented the nonvoluntary collection of biometrics from Afghan citizens in most situations. I did an initial inquiry but no one could tell me specifically what the policy said, when it had been promulgated, or by whom, or if this was the result of some kind of bilateral (U.S.–Afghan) or legal based decision making. The more I heard about it, the more flakey the whole thing seemed, so I started going through SOPs, orders, and policies issued by past RC East commanders, and eventually I found a document called FRAGO 41 that had been issued by a previous RC East commander at least three years earlier. However, the document was not even about biometrics and certainly did not state anything about which I had been told. I did find other guidance regarding biometrics collections that advised, but did not mandate, voluntary collection of biometrics from Afghans not believed to be involved in violent incidents. But even here it did not appear that this policy was the result of any discussions held between the U.S. military and the Afghan government, nor was it specifically linked to any other bilateral agreements or legal statutes. It may just have been someone's good idea at the time and never reexamined.

## EFFECTIVE POLICY ENABLES EFFECTIVE BIOMETRICS OPERATIONS

Planning for biometrics operations should also involve assessing the current policy environment to ensure that existing policies support the collection, use, and sharing of biometric data within our area of operations. In my experience, the absence of policies that specifically authorize biometrics to be collected from individuals in a mission area can have nearly as negative an impact on the military use of biometrics as policies that specifically forbid biometrics collection. I'm not sure exactly why this is, but it may be in part due to concerns over legal or privacy issues and the general lack of familiarity with the technology. It may also be due in part to the fact that many of the soldiers and Marines we want to do the collecting would rather be doing something other than lugging around another piece of equipment that often seems to have no immediate impact on their mission. For these reasons, it is very important to have specific policies

**Figure 3.2** These two photos show the biometric enrollment of temporary day-workers outside a coalition base in Iraq. Despite initial policy constraints, the Coalition eventually devised a method to biometrically screen the thousands of temporary local national workers who accessed our bases every day.

authorizing (or even mandating) the execution of a robust biometric collection program.

Even when formal biometrics policies have been adopted, they may have as many negative impacts as positive, and the law of unintended consequences often comes into effect. When former LTC Vinny Johns was helping to field the BISA systems in Iraq in 2005, he noticed that policies that may have been intended to aid in the collection of biometrics in one set of circumstances could actually have the opposite effect in another application. For example, the Coalition policy at the time stated that all local or third country national employees serving on formal contracts supporting the military had to be vetted and biometrically enrolled. But since it did not specifically address collecting biometrics from the tens of thousands of completely unvetted workers (known as "day workers") hired on a daily basis to do all kind of jobs in and around Coalition facilities (Figure 3.2), many Coalition officials interpreted that as meaning you could *not* collect such data. Vinny spent many frustrating months trying to get this policy gap closed because, as he explained to me: "Our policy defeated our system." Clearly, anticipating and addressing such policy gaps need to be part of planning and preparing for biometrics operations.

## TTPs AND TRAINING

It is no surprise that when we first started using biometrics in combat, we had not developed operational processes for how we should employ this new capability. It's also not surprising that we did not initially have effective training programs. What is surprising is that when I deployed to Afghanistan in 2009, our operations were still hampered by the lack of standardized processes and by inadequate training. Operating a system like a BAT kit can be taught to the user fairly quickly. The user can also be provided a manual, or even a "smart card," that describes how to put the system into operation, how to download and upload data, and how to sync with other devices like the HIIDE. However, teaching his sergeant, platoon leader, or company commander how and where to employ his biometrics capability for maximum effect is far more complicated but as critical to the overall effectiveness of the mission.*

Preparing a force to employ a new technical capability like biometrics as a battlefield tool requires the development of operational Tactics, Techniques and Procedures (TTPs), as well as effective training programs to teach these TTPs to the individuals *and* units that will employ these capabilities on the battlefield (many/most for the first time). While the Marines seemed to appreciate this need early on, the Army, for the most part, did appear to be as on board.† Training for individual system operators did occur during predeployment exercises at the Joint Readiness Training Center, but there was no unit level training (i.e., collective training).‡ This pattern continued after unit deployment, where, for the most part, only basic system-operator training was provided by the theater biometrics organizations in Iraq and Afghanistan.§ As I noted in my "Foreword," there was also no concerted effort to capture and publish anything approaching joint operational doctrine or standardized TTPs upon which such training could be based. The result is, in my opinion (supported by GAO, Government Accountability Office, assessments), that our ability to take full advantage of the potential of biometrics was

* In my interview with Crossmatch SEEK trainer Tony Cyprian, he told me that he always began any training effort by training a unit's junior leaders before he conducted training for actual system operators. This approach not only ensured that leaders understood how to employ biometrics but also that they were capable of supervising the efforts of the system operators.

† The Marines followed up their initial exposure to biometrics in Iraq in 2004 with the purchase of over 200 BAT systems, which they used at Camp Pendleton to train units preparing for upcoming combat deployments.

‡ There were also no observer-controllers trained in biometrics who could advise and evaluate units during their tactical training events.

§ The biometrics organization in Iraq eventually developed a more robust program of biometrics training for newly arrived personnel, but it was for individuals, not units or leaders, and was not mandatory.

significantly degraded.* Future biometric operations need to be supported by effective TTP development and adequate training, both of which will go a long way to offsetting any technical deficiencies that may exist.†

## COLLECTION CONSIDERATIONS

Assuming that adequate planning and preparation have occurred, once an operation has begun, it is vital to exploit all opportunities to conduct biometric collection activities. To be truly effective, biometric collections should be performed not only in direct support of a specific military activity (e.g., base access control, offensive operations, personnel vetting, etc.), but also at *every* possible point in which the United States or allied forces come into contact with the local populace. For example, biometrics should be collected whenever dispensing aid, providing medical services, or training local/host nation security forces. These collections will support military and humanitarian activities by reducing fraud, regulating the delivery of medicines and other resources, and ensuring that training is not provided to criminals or other suspect individuals. These collections would also help to increase the size and scope of the biometrics database. Unfortunately, such a common sense and holistic approach to collecting biometric data was not employed to maximum effect through most of the last decade of war, primarily because there was a lack of the vision and authority to make it happen.

* In its April 2012 report, the Government Accountability Office stated that, "biometrics training for leaders does not provide detailed instructions on how to effectively use and manage biometrics collection tools," and the result of this deficiency was that "military personnel are limited in their ability to collect high-quality biometrics data to better confirm the identity of enemy combatants."

† I could have written an entire chapter just about training issues. When I returned to the United States from Afghanistan, I went immediately to Joint Readiness Training Center (JRTC) at Fort Polk, LA to discuss biometrics training for predeploying forces and observe some of the training in action. What I saw confirmed previous assessments about the inadequacy of our biometric training efforts for deploying forces. I spent the next six months or so trying to push the Army to develop better training, particularly for units and leaders—an effort that met with only partial success. Hampering the effort to improve training was the lack of any guidance from the U.S. Central Command (CENTCOM) regarding predeployment biometrics training. There were dozens of required joint training tasks for individuals and units deploying to the CENTCOM area but none for biometrics. I eventually put together a short list and sent it to the CENTCOM Biometrics office, but I am not sure if they were ever put into formal usage.

Quality and completeness of collection are two key areas that also need to be maximized whenever possible. Different collection systems will have different image capture capabilities. So, all things being equal, using the highest quality sensors available will help ensure that the biometrics database has the highest quality data possible. This can be critical when trying to match directly captured fingerprints against partial or latent prints, for example. Of course, forces conducting mobile combat operations may not always have the choice of which systems to use and may not be operating in environments conducive to the careful collection of biometrics; however, if it is possible to reenroll suspect or detained individuals, using better equipment and in a controlled environment, then this is what should be done. Never just settle for inferior collections because inferior collections yield inferior results.

Policies on what kinds of biometrics to collect will vary based upon the type of operation, available equipment, and local commanders' directives. Over the past few years, the U.S. military operating in Iraq and Afghanistan generally conducted two main types of enrollments: full and hasty. A full enrollment using a standard multimodel system like a BAT or HIIDE normally included at least three facial photos (frontal and both profiles), two iris images, and all 10 digits (fingers and thumbs) with slap and rolled prints, if possible. Some systems, such as the Biometrics Identification System for Access (BISA) used in Iraq, also captured palm prints, although the DoD did not have the ability to match that modality at the time. I have also seen some Marine Corps documents that described collecting the edge of the hand (aka the "Knife Edge").* The assumption in performing a full enrollment is that you have a fairly controlled environment, a fairly controlled target population, and a suitable amount of time in which to perform your task. Enrollments for base access or during detention are two examples of such environments.† It may also be possible to collect additional modalities in such environments, such as DNA or the previously mentioned palm prints.

Most collections by operating forces will not occur in such controlled environments, however, and that's where the hasty enrollment process

* A number of systems being currently marketed for the law enforcement mission use the term "writer's palm" to refer to the capture and matching of latent prints from the side of the hand.

† One of other comments from my interviews with Vinny Johns worth highlighting was that the equipment used to enroll individuals for base access produced consistently high quality biometric images, which had a positive impact on the overall quality of the DoD database and thus had a positive impact on the entire biometric effort.

comes in. Although policies differ, a hasty enrollment is usually described as including at least one front angle face picture, both irises, and at least the thumb and forefingers of each hand. A hasty enrollment policy needs to be flexible enough to allow for additional data to be collected, if possible, and to focus on the population most likely to be of interest (i.e., military-aged males). It is important for the local commander to realize that while a hasty enrollment is better than nothing, it should always be the goal to find a way to improve upon this minimal (and perhaps lower quality) collection, particularly if we are dealing with a population likely to represent a current or potential threat.

Like any military activity, biometric collection operations need to be well-planned-for in advance. Biometrics collection planning considerations should include the impact of the location, the modalities to be collected, security considerations, the matching mechanism to be employed (to include planning for uploading current watchlist data), and above all, communications. Collections will often be regulated by the theater or local commander's policies, which may in turn, be influenced by the host nation's laws (where applicable) and the cultural norms of the local populace. It is always important to take the attitudes of the local populace into account, and, in many cases, integrating members of the host nation or local security forces into the conduct of biometrics collections will help ameliorate any negative perceptions by those targeted for collection. For example, U.S. forces operating in both Iraq and Afghanistan found it very useful to engage with local leadership and the local security or militia forces in planning for biometrics collections. In fact, we were sometimes able to convince local village leaders that collecting biometrics on military-aged males in their villages and providing those enrolled with some kind of identity card could help deter outsiders from entering their villages and disrupting the local power structure (or making the village a possible target for future kinetic operations by U.S. or Coalition forces). The bottom line is that it is always better to involve local officials or security elements in biometrics collections than to go it alone. Providing an incentive to cooperate (or a disincentive, if they do not cooperate) can be very useful in securing local cooperation.*

* The relationship between a local population and the government authorities should be considered before deciding how much to involve the latter in the biometrics collection process. There are many parts of Afghanistan where anyone other than a local tribal leader or village elder would be looked upon as representing an imposed outside authority.

## THE MODALITY SHOULD MATCH THE MISSION

One of the questions that frequently comes up in any discussion of military biometrics uses is: "What is the best modality?" Unfortunately, the most accurate answer, and one that may not always be completely satisfying, is: "It depends." Every commonly used modality has at least some value, dependent upon the mission it is supporting and the operational environment (see Table 3.2). There are also negative aspects of each that need to be considered before employing any biometrics system. Each modality can be judged by a number of factors, including accuracy, speed (both of collection and comparison/matching), collectability, and others, but it really comes down to determining what is best for the mission and the environment in which the mission is being executed. Iris images are easily collected, highly accurate, and can be rapidly matched against a large database, but they are of little use when the requirement is to match new collections against biometrics left at crime scenes or on captured enemy material (like improvised explosive device components), because iris images are not left at such locations. Similarly, facial recognition has great potential to identify individuals from a distance and without their knowledge, but it is not nearly as accurate as fingerprints or iris images and will not help if the targeted individual is a burka-wearing female in the Middle East (or someone masquerading as a burka-wearing female). DNA may be the only way to identify a "successful" suicide bomber, but the complexity, expense, and time required to collect and process a DNA sample makes it much less useful for most tactical/operational applications.* The bottom line is that, all things being equal, the decision on which modality to focus when collecting biometrics needs to be driven by a keen understanding of the target population, the operational environment, and the mission and capabilities of the friendly force (see Appendix B for more information on biometric modalities).

To illustrate the issue of modality selection from my own personal experience, I'll use an incident that occurred during my deployment to Afghanistan during the summer of 2009. As part of the "surge" that was begun at the time, the U.S. Marines deployed a number of brigades and supporting units to Helmand Province. The supporting elements included a biometrics management component to provide support to Marine operations. Although the Marines had deployed with the standard collection

* A previously cited RAND Corp. study published in 2010 recommended that DNA should only be used for "for narrow, targeted applications" and called for more research into the applications and implications of a wider use of DNA for battlefield identity management.

**Table 3.2** Operational Considerations for Modality Selection

| Modality | Optimal Uses | Remarks |
|---|---|---|
| Fingerprint | • Tactical ID<br>• Force protection<br>• Forensics | + Large and plentiful datasets for potential matching<br>+ Commonly left at crime scenes, attack sites, and on enemy equipment and documents<br>– Large file-size (for full enrollment) may limit storage on handheld devices<br>– Print quality can be negatively affected by environmental factors and training<br>– Enrollment and matching process can be slow |
| Facial Recognition | • Visual verification[a]<br>• Stand-off threat detection<br>• Surveillance<br>• Intelligence<br>• Video/photo forensics | + Can be collected at a distance and covertly<br>+ May be able to match images against large commercial or intelligence datasets for intelligence or investigative purposes<br>– Match accuracy low against larger datasets<br>– Image quality highly affected by distance, camera/lens, and environmental factors<br>– Face angle, pose, and lighting complicate matching |
| Iris | • Access control[b]<br>• Population management<br>• Detainee management | + Very accurate matching against large datasets<br>+ Fast and simple collection<br>+ Small enrollment file size maximizes storage capabilities for handheld devices<br>+ Increasingly used for border/immigration control, national and voter ID<br>– Most criminal and military biometrics databases are predominantly fingerprint-based |

*(Continued)*

**Table 3.2 (*Continued*)** Operational Considerations for Modality Selection

| Modality | Optimal Uses | Remarks |
|---|---|---|
| DNA | • Forensics<br>• Intelligence | + Highly accurate<br>+ Usually left at crime/attack scenes and on materials<br>+ Can indicate familial connections, and individual-specific genetic markers and environmental information<br>– Slow, complicated, and resource-intensive to process<br>– Processing and matching usually requires a lab facility<br>– Subject to sample degradation and contamination |
| Palm | • Forensics | + Often left at crime/attack scenes and on materials<br>– Automated and manual matching can be difficult<br>– Limited datasets available for matching |

[a] Facial images can be also effective for visual identity verification when automated matching is not available.

[b] This assumes a complete enrollment, in which fingerprint collection has already been accomplished.

systems (BAT and HIIDE), they soon began looking for alternative capabilities that would be easier to employ. At one point, the Biometrics Task Force at Bagram Airbase got word that the Marines were considering deploying a couple of hundred Pier iris collection devices, which had proved very useful in their population management efforts in Iraq's western Al-Anbar Province. The problem was that while the Pier is an excellent and fairly small device that is simple to use, it only collects iris images. As I previously stated, iris images are not useful in connecting individuals to IED events, which are the principal killers of U.S. and Coalition personnel in Afghanistan, nor can they be matched against the vast bulk of biometric data collected by both the military and international law enforcement agencies, which are based almost totally upon fingerprints. We were eventually able to convince the Marines that the Pier would be a great tool for identity verification in a mission such as a population management, but only AFTER doing a full enrollment of the local populace, which included fingerprint collections. However, iris image collection alone would not be operationally effective when encountering a new/unknown individual or someone suspected of involvement in IED-related activities.

## THE IMPACT OF THE COALITION OPERATIONS

If you think it sounds complicated to make all of this work within the U.S. military, there are additional complications when conducting biometric operations with and alongside foreign military partners. As our recent history has shown, military actions of almost any size will normally involve working with foreign forces, and this was particularly the case in Afghanistan.

Each of the nations in ISAF brought with them a different approach to biometrics, from the complete lack of any capability to deploying forces with their own biometrics systems. While the United States could not possibly provide equipment and training to allow all of our unprepared coalition allies to conduct their own biometric operations, it was necessary to provide at least some capability to many of them, particularly those operating most closely with U.S. forces. It was also important to help maximize biometrics collections across the ISAF coalition and to ensure that insurgents and terrorists were not able to find "identity sanctuaries" where they could operate with a reduced chance of detection. Such a situation creates seams between allies that can put our own forces at additional risk when these anonymous actors operate in our own areas as well.

It might seem that having allies with their own biometrics capabilities would be preferable to having those with none at all, but this is not always the case. For example, when our British allies deployed with biometrics systems, they were invariably ones that were incompatible with our own, which necessitated complex technical and procedural workarounds in order to be able to share collected data and watchlists. In addition, some of our ISAF allies had significant constraints, both cultural and legal, to sharing or even collecting biometrics data from foreign persons. A number of our European allies also had privacy and legal policies (some less formal than others) that made them extremely hesitant to collect biometrics from Afghans and to share their collected information with U.S. forces, if that data might also be used by U.S. law enforcement or intelligence agencies. In many cases, resolving these policy differences was arguably more difficult than addressing technical issues.

Planning to address Coalition complications in advance of military operations would have obviously been preferable, but in the absence of such planning, U.S. forces in Afghanistan had to do what U.S. forces do in every military operation—improvise. In many cases, this improvisation took the shape of providing U.S. equipment directly to our closest partners for joint biometrics operations. In these cases, U.S. military personnel, equipped with U.S. communications equipment, were often able to transmit the collected data and pass on any match results to the allied unit. In other cases, the biometrics data might be collected by the foreign military unit and copied to a storage medium like a CD (compact disc) and then transported to a U.S. unit for transmission over U.S. communications networks. Eventually, the establishment of a Coalition-wide communications network for Afghanistan made data transmissions easier and timelier.

Addressing the legal and policy issues was often more complicated than technical concerns, as previously noted. In some cases, fairly complex bilateral data-sharing agreements were drawn up between the United States and partner nations. These agreements often specified the kind of biometrics data that could be collected, what it could be used for, how long it could be retained (particularly after the mission was complete), and with whom it could be shared. In some cases, certain countries did not want us to share their data with certain other countries. In other instances, some countries were opposed to their collected data being shared with U.S. domestic law enforcement.

During my time in Afghanistan, the United States and a number of our closest allies in the ISAF Coalition began working on a project to establish a separate Coalition biometrics database. In order to address the political and legal concerns of Coalition members, there were also to be technical and procedural protections (i.e., business rules) in place, which would give each nation submitting biometrics data control over who else within the Coalition could access their data and how matches would be reported across the Coalition. There were also to be rules that would govern the disposition of a country's biometrics data, once that country ended its participation in ISAF.*

One of the early supporting actions to this project was to have each participating nation submit its legal and privacy policies regarding military use of biometrics, in order that a full understanding of the impacts upon the biometrics system could be understood. This apparently straightforward effort proved very difficult in practice, since most countries did not, in fact, have laws or policies specifically dealing with biometric collection or data sharing, particularly in the context of military operations (this included the United States). In the end, the ISAF leadership declined to endorse the project, despite the fact that the overall concept was sound and despite the approval for much of the required funding. I'll discuss this more in Appendix E.

The lesson from the above is the same point I have made elsewhere in this chapter, which is that advanced planning for biometrics operations is essential. Planning for a Coalition operation involving biometrics requires understanding the technical capabilities that each nation brings to the fight, as well as the legal and sometimes cultural impacts that may affect their use of biometrics. We should also understand what biometric data they may already have that could be useful in developing our operational database and if they have their own data-sharing agreements with other countries, which may be of use to the Coalition mission as a whole. The bottom line is, we should know all of these things BEFORE the operation begins so that we can build the appropriate procedures (both technical and operational) and the required policies that will support the maximum employment of biometrics capabilities across the coalition.

## THE SIX Ps: PRIOR PLANNING PREVENTS PISS-POOR PERFORMANCE

Early in my army career, we had an Army Chief of Staff who was focused on preparing the force for the first engagement with the enemy and who

* Each country's data was to be stored in separate but linked repositories. At the end of its involvement with ISAF, each country could leave its data in place, withdraw the data for its own national purposes (e.g., border or immigration control), or have the data deleted.

stated that we should have no more "Task Force Smiths."* Unfortunately, decades later, when we first started using the new technology of biometrics on the battlefield of Afghanistan and Iraq, we were not well prepared. That is understandable, because this technology was, in a word, "new." What is truly disheartening is that for most of the next decade we continued to spend many millions of dollars on equipment that we often put in the hands of relatively untrained soldiers and units without the development of proper procedures and policies on how to use the new technology, without detailed mechanisms to support operating with our allies, and without adequate supporting communications infrastructure and procedures. These shortcomings must be addressed before we engage in our next major combat operation, but history is not very kind in that regard.

In order to illustrate the concepts I've discussed here, and will discuss in the next few chapters, I've constricted a scenario which will begin below and continue over the next four chapters. It is intended to provide a clear depiction of how a major combat operation can be properly supported by biometrics.

* Task Force Smith was the first unit to deploy to South Korea, from occupation duties in Japan, after the invasion by the North. With poorly trained and poorly equipped soldiers, it confronted a North Korean armored column south of Seoul and was brushed aside by communists as they headed south.

# 4

# Biometrics Support to Offensive Operations

Now that we have examined how to use the intelligence process to link previously collected biometrics with intelligence information, to develop profiles/dossiers of threat personalities or other persons of interest (PoIs), and to add those individuals assessed as posing the greatest threat to a biometrically enabled watchlist, how can we use this fusion of biometrics and intelligence? In a combat operation, the principal use of biometrics will likely be to identify the enemy and his supporters. Using biometrics to support offensive operations—from targeted operations, like kill/capture raids, to operations that support control of an area of operations through population management activities—helps ensure that we focus our often limited resources in ways that maximize their utility while helping to avoid unnecessary negative consequences. You don't have to be a bleeding heart to realize that killing or capturing the wrong people not only wastes our resources (bullets, bombs, soldiers, facilities, and time), but also often alienates the local populace. This alienation can result in a range of negative reactions from the absence of human intelligence reporting to the generation of a cycle of retaliatory violence by the relatives or friends of those affected by our operations. This was certainly the case in the early days of the Iraq war when U.S. forces often seemed to simply vacuum up all the military-aged males in a particular village during operations and then tried to sort them out in overcrowded and poorly managed detention facilities like the infamous Abu Ghraib.

## ATTACKING THE NETWORK

Prior to 9/11, U.S. forces and, in particular, U.S. military intelligence personnel were trained to focus on the kinds of enemy forces that were organized into a similar unit-based structure and hierarchy. Operations in Iraq and Afghanistan caused us to face a new threat—the networked threat. Insurgent and terrorist groups tended to be organized more like criminal networks than like military forces. That was especially true with regard to the threat from Improvised Explosive Devices or IEDs. The U.S. military's initial reaction to what was to become the biggest killer of its personnel in both wars was to attempt to beat that threat with technology and firepower. However, unlike a conventional military force, the networked threat could modify techniques, tactics, and systems much faster than we could; so an effort began to make the counter-IED (CIED) fight more proactive by attacking the networks themselves instead of just trying to defeat the devices.*

Being able to identify the members of the IED networks in Afghanistan was of particular interest to units assigned to perform "route clearance" (RC) missions (Figure 4.1). These engineer units were responsible for ensuring that major lines of communications in the theater of combat were free of roadside bombs, which were the greatest killers of our forces and which often disrupted the movement of units and logistics. Without the ability to understand and attack the IED networks before an attack, the job of the RC units often seemed to be driving around waiting to get blown up, which they often did. As a result, RC forces had a definite interest in the collection of biometrics and were often some of the most aggressive collectors within the conventional (i.e., non-SOF) force. Route clearance engineers became skilled at exploiting IED sites, whether those were sites of bombings, locations of IEDs discovered before detonations, or cache sites containing IED-making materials. They also became adept at the direct collection of biometrics from local nationals detained in conjunction with IED attacks or who happened to be in the area of an attack or where bombs were located before detonation.

* The initial reaction to the IED threat was to put bigger and better armor on our tactical vehicles and to employ a variety of technical and tactical countermeasures to detect IEDs, to intercept and interrupt the radio signals that were often used to trigger the explosive devices, and to attack the triggermen. It soon became clear that this—essentially reactive—tactic was not eliminating the threat, which led to efforts to detect, degrade, and destroy the networks of insurgents who were building and emplacing the IEDs before they could be used in an effort described as "left of boom." The tactics used to do this eventually became known collectively as "attack the network."

**Figure 4.1** Members of an army route clearance unit collect biometrics from an Afghan villager.

## BIOMETRICALLY ENABLED CHECKPOINT OPERATIONS

Establishing a checkpoint (CP) in an area of operations may not seem like a particularly offensive type of activity; yet, CPs can be an important tool in support of ongoing offensive operations or in support of future offensive operations. Checkpoints can also assist in the key counterinsurgency effort of population management (also known as population control). Providing the checkpoint with a biometric collection system, which includes an up-to-date biometric watchlist, makes the CP much more likely to find the bad actors for whom we are looking or to drive the enemy where we want them to go, or to more effectively map the human terrain. All CPs should be equipped with a biometric collection capability whenever possible.

Any offensive operation against a specific objective, whether it be a capture/kill operation to isolate and search a particular location (often a small town or village) directed against a specific individual or individuals, a raid, or a cordon operation, is going to have to deal with possible "leakers" trying to escape the objective area on foot or in a vehicle. A well-planned and tactically situated CP, or series of CPs, can help friendly forces identify and detain the wanted individuals or their previously identified associates, who are attempting to elude the operation. Biometrically-enabled IPB analysis can help determine the best places to locate such CPs throughout the area of operations. If time and the operational situation permit, personnel manning a checkpoint can enroll all individuals, or at least a representative subset such as military-aged males, passing through the area. Even if this action does not result in the identification or detention of threat personnel or other PoIs, it could provide important information for use in the intelligence process.

Occasionally, the tactical situation may call for the establishment of an unplanned or hasty CP (also called "Snap CPs") in order to isolate a particular area or prevent the escape of personnel as just described. Ensuring that such missions are assigned to units equipped with a biometrics capability will maximize their effectiveness, partially if such actions are anticipated and directed as "on call" missions in the operations plan. This could be especially useful if biometrics collection devices are not available to the entire force. Establishing an element of trained collectors that could be deployed as the tactical situation dictates can partially make up for equipment or operator shortages.

Establishing checkpoints with biometrics may also provide support for future offensive operations by helping to control the movement of threat elements or by providing the information that can lead to more accurate and efficient operations against threat individuals and organizations. CPs can definitely have an effect on the movement of threat personnel, particularly if employed over time in a particular area. For example, if we know that threat elements use a particular border crossing that we may not control or where we may not be able to target them, we could establish a routine of establishing biometrics-enabled CPs along the main route(s) leading away from the crossing point, which may serve to divert the movement of our targets to another area where we can engage them more effectively. This will be especially effective if we have successfully used biometrics to identify and capture individuals in the area in the past.

## BIOMETRICS FOR POPULATION MANAGEMENT

At the tactical level, operations designed to control or manage a local population can be vital to cutting the ties that bind the insurgent to the local populace, which afford the insurgent support and allow him/her to hide. In previous counterinsurgency campaigns, such as those in Vietnam and Malaysia, one key tactic used to isolate the local populace from the insurgents was to relocate the former into protected villages (known as the "Strategic Hamlets" in Vietnam). While this tactic can be effective, particularly when these villages are provided adequate support and protection, it is expensive and can lead to serious resentment by the populace who are forced to evacuate their homes and farms. In Iraq, a number of commanders attempted to isolate the populace from the insurgents within their towns or villages through the use of barriers, checkpoints, and the registration of the local population, which included biometrics enrollment. This tactic was used very effectively in the city of Fallujah after the second campaign to rid the town of insurgents was conducted in late 2004.* After combat operations successfully eliminated the insurgent presence there, the population was temporarily evacuated and the city surrounded by a series of barriers, with the exception of a few guarded access points. Before the populace was allowed back into the city, all military-aged males were biometrically enrolled, registered, and given ID cards. These cards and the collected biometric data were used to verify the identities of these individuals when reentering the city and during spot checks by roving patrols within the city itself, which helped prevent the reinfiltration of insurgents into the city as had occurred after the First Battle of Fallujah earlier in the year. These tactics helped end the insurgents' use of Fallujah as a staging ground for attacks in Baghdad and in Al Anbar province.

Population control efforts in Afghanistan were much less widespread, given the dispersal of the population into smaller and often remote villages and the smaller U.S. and Allied military presence in much of the country. Moreover, Afghans tended to be more fiercely independent of any outside control than their counterparts in Iraq and, thus, even discussion of terms such as "population control" was not encouraged.

## SCENARIO: OFFENSIVE BIOMETRICS

A team of collectors using mobile BATs and HIIDEs would accompany the main force entering the village and perform hasty enrollments (face, both index fingers and thumbs, and both irises) on any males encountered and full enrollments on any locals who were detained. A small site exploitation team from the Task Force, using the newly acquired Advanced Biometrics Collection Device (ABCD), would also accompany the main

* Originally described in Chapter 1.

force to collect biometrics, including latent prints and DNA from any IED components found in the area or from captured enemy documents.

The raid went off rather as planned. Biometrics collections at the checkpoints identified a number of suspected fighters whose fingerprints matched latent prints found at attack sites and at weapons caches over the previous weeks. Additional identifications, including one suspected militant who matched to a collection taken from a group of police trainees in the prior month, were made within the village itself. The exploitation team collected high-quality latent prints from weapons and IED materials using the ABCD, which was able to make immediate enrollment-quality digital images from the latent prints and to share them wirelessly with other biometrics collectors on the mission. This enabled immediate matches to the latents to be made to a number of the military-aged males who had been enrolled in the village. Although matching using latent prints had not been done before with a handheld device, the results using the ABCD were considered to have enough certainty to permit U.S. forces to temporarily detain the identified individuals while further analysis was done by latent print examiners at the AFRICOM IdRes forward element in Djibouti.* Two of these latent print matches were subsequently confirmed, and the individuals in question were moved to the theater detention facility at the Task Force headquarters as per the Operation's Rules of Engagement.

* This process was specific to the advanced capability present in the ABCD and was included in the mission's biometric rules of engagement.

# 5

# Biometrics Support for Defensive Operations

We have seen how biometrics can help us find and positively identify the bad guys and other persons of interest, but how do we use these same capabilities when the bad guys come looking for us? Biometrics have probably played as important a role, or maybe more so, in protecting our forces and resources from enemy actions and criminal mischief, as it has in allowing us to conduct more accurate and efficient offensive operations. Employing biometrics as part of any vetting process could help ensure that we do not hire, train, support, or pay individuals who participate in or support insurgents or terrorist groups or criminal organizations. Biometrics is also well suited to providing the extra security to control access to resources of all kinds—from facilities, to supplies, to computer networks. Finally, biometrics can provide an extra layer of protection for forces operating in the field, whether they are conducting combat missions, performing humanitarian tasks, or engaging with local officials.

This chapter will address the following key concepts:

- The integration of biometrics into access control systems is vital to the effective protection of friendly personnel, resources, and facilities.
- Vetting of local nationals for hiring, contracting for services, or training, must include the collection and use of biometric data.
- Biometrics can aid in insider threat detection.

- Biometric-enabled checkpoints or the use of biometrics by screening forces provide more robust force protection for friendly forces during combat operations.

## BIOMETRICS FOR ACCESS CONTROL

Biometrics have been used to secure government and civilian facilities in the United States and abroad, but only relatively recently has it found a role in helping to protect deployed military forces. In Chapter 1, I described the impact that the Mosul DFAC attack had on spurring the employment of biometrics for base access control throughout the region. In Iraq (and also elsewhere in the Southwest Asia region), a base access system called the Biometric Identification System for Access (BISA) was widely deployed and used to help vet and screen non-U.S. personnel requesting access to U.S.-run facilities (more on that later) for the purposes of employment, provision of supplies and services, and/or for operational reasons (Figure 5.1). BISA also had the ability to create and

**Figure 5.1** BISA base access system used in Iraq. BISA is the only biometrics base access control system specifically developed for deployed military forces.

**Figure 5.2** BATs used for access control at Bagram Airbase, Afghanistan. The BAT system was used to vet and screen nonmilitary personnel entering most of the larger Coalition bases in Afghanistan.

print a biometrically-enabled access badge, which helped speed the entry for those individuals who required regular access to a base. Smaller facilities in Iraq, as well as most U.S.-controlled bases in Afghanistan, used other biometrics systems, normally the previously described Biometric Automated Toolset (BAT) (Figure 5.2). Even though not typically considered an access control system, the BAT has been used in that role almost since its inception and has performed adequately.* Some of the smallest "bases" or combat outposts (COPs) even used the HIIDE (Handheld Interagency Identity Detection Equipment) to screen individuals entering their areas.

In order to be truly effective, a biometric access control system should be able to exchange data with the biometrics systems being used by operational forces. Data collected in the field must be available to support access-control decision making, and access-control data should, similarly,

* See Appendix C for more information on the BAT, including its history.

be accessible to operational forces to help them establish the identities of individuals they encounter in the field. This data exchange is not always as easy as it seems.

It is also very important that an access control system should have the ability to use the same biometric watchlist being used by forces in the field since this access will normally provide the fastest and most reliable way to immediately identify and screen out the individuals who present the greatest threat to our forces and facilities. Once again, this may not always be technically feasible.

Base protection and access control are obviously critical for any military force, but particularly so when that force is operating in an environment in which attacks or other threats are likely to occur. In many of the places where the United States and its allies are currently conducting military operations, they are doing so with less than optimal protection since there is no biometrics access control system designed specifically for tactical/deployed forces. The previously mentioned BISA system is no longer in use and the BAT, which was not designed as an access-control system, is not a viable long-term answer. Unfortunately, there are no plans within the U.S. Department of Defense to acquire a system for biometrics base control for deployed forces, and there does not appear to be much incentive within industry to offer such a capability. However, I firmly believe that such a capability is a requirement that cannot be overlooked. Such a system would have the following features:

1. Ability to collect multiple modalities: Face, finger, and iris, at a minimum
2. Ability to operate high-quality biometric sensors for initial enrollment
3. Ability to provide a mobile/remote screening capability using a handheld device
4. Ability to operate on either unclassified or classified networks
5. Ability to use a watchlist
6. Ability to produce a badge to facilitate identity verifications for individuals requiring regular access

## BIOMETRICS SUPPORT FOR PERSONAL VETTING

Contrary to popular belief, modern military forces do not arrive on the battlefield or in the operational area with everything they need to conduct sustained operations. In fact, in any operation of more than a few days in length, significant external support will be required, particularly in the areas of logistics, transportation, and base services, and the need for this support will grow as the duration of the operation increases. In many cases, this support will come from individuals and organizations that are not only outside the military but are from outside of the United States as well. And often, this support will need to come from the population in the area of operations, which, in the case of a COIN operation, is likely to be the same population from which the insurgents draw their members and supporters. Obviously, this dependence upon external elements presents a significant security risk.

Every military operation needs to have a comprehensive force protection plan that includes a process for vetting foreign personnel with whom a deployed force will come into contact. Knowing who among this army of foreign contractors or other support personnel is friend or foe is an absolutely critical component of any force protection program. The less we can trust the local government to provide accurate and verifiable information on the personnel, who we must hire or with whom we must do business, the greater is the need for a robust personnel vetting program, which must include the use of biometrics. In a place like Afghanistan, where there are few repositories of official and/or reliable personal information, establishing a person's true identity is problematic, particularly in the more remote areas. Without a tool like biometrics, a decision about whether or not a potential local hire (aka Locally Employed Person, or LEP) is a threat may rest solely upon hearsay, such as when a local leader vouches for a cousin, nephew, or tribe member. With biometrics, we can know if the individual's fingerprints or DNA have been discovered at sites or on material associated with attacks or were otherwise found on captured enemy documents or equipment. We may also be able to tell if the individual was previously employed at another facility and then fired because of suspicious actions or criminal activity.* If we are operating in a country where the local police forces use fingerprinting, we may also be able to compare our vetting enrollments to the local or national law enforcement database to determine if the prospective hire has a local criminal record.†

* Which can prevent an activity known as "FOB hopping," whereby an individual is barred from access to one Forward Operating Base or FOB and then attempts to get access to another base in the vicinity, often using an assumed name. Preventing this was one of the earliest missions for biometric systems deployed to the Balkans in the late 1990s.

† Unless we have already gotten access to the data beforehand, as described in Chapter 2.

### PERSONAL VIGNETTE ON THE VALUE OF BIOMETRIC VETTING

During one of my first days in Afghanistan, I was in the TF Biometrics Intelligence hut when a match report came in regarding a prospective LEP whose fingerprints matched to latent prints found on some IED components a few years earlier. When we contacted the FOB (Forward Operating Base) intelligence officer, his initial response was something like "he seems okay" and that they would "keep an eye on him." He eventually accepted our argument that this fingerprint match was a near certainty, at which point he agreed to take action. Only biometrics could have successfully and definitively linked this individual to his "hidden past."

Biometric vetting should not just apply to individuals who will be working on our bases but should also apply to those who provide support for our forces from outside of our facilities. Unfortunately, biometrics has not always been used to vet or screen local nationals who are providing critical and costly support but are not seeking base access. While in Afghanistan, I discovered that there was a significant gap in the theater policy with regard to the vetting of local persons who won contracts to provide services for our forces or facilities. One such individual of whom I became aware owned a company that won a contract to perform about US$1 million worth of work on one of our isolated outposts near the Torkham Gate border crossing. According to our intelligence team, the business owner was suspected of being an insurgent financier. I did a bit of quick research and learned that there was no vetting requirement (biometrics or otherwise) within ISAF (International Security Assistance Forces) for the owners of companies that won service contracts. As a result of this failure to properly screen local business owners, it is quite possible that at least some of the money we paid these people ended up supporting the insurgency. A better policy, and one that I learned had been in effect previously in Iraq, was for all successful bidders for U.S. contracts over a specific dollar figure to have their senior personnel (not just the workers who ended up on our facilities) subjected to CI, criminal, and biometric vetting processes.

Another significant gap in personnel vetting that came to light sometime later involved employees of the numerous local security companies that were hired to provide external security for ISAF facilities and to protect the movement of logistics convoys across the country. In the fall of 2009, the Government of Afghanistan (GoA) announced that it was taking action to bring these groups under some kind of government control. As part of this effort, the government officials requested that ISAF assist them in biometrically enrolling these armed security personnel, most of whom had never had biometrics collected from them—even those that were carrying weapons in the vicinity of U.S. and allied forces. The main reason given by the GoA for this request was that the protocol was to ensure that these security companies were not training and arming members of the insurgency but also (and perhaps of greater interest to senior GoA leaders) to ensure that members of the Afghan security forces were not "double dipping" by serving as higher paid civilian guards while also receiving their government paychecks.

In any counterinsurgency operation, building the capacity of the host nation security forces is critical. Training local law enforcement, security, and military forces is often necessary to get them to the level where they can augment and work with the U.S. and its allies and eventually replace them. However, as indicated above, it is vitally important that we are not training members or supporters of the insurgency. Even in training missions that are not part of an active COIN effort, such as many of the peacetime training efforts our military undertakes across the globe, it is important that we do not train terrorists, members of criminal organizations, or those who may have committed atrocities or other human rights abuses against civilians. Not only is it bad business to train bad people, but the revelation of these activities can often have a dramatic impact on our defense and foreign policies. Thus, a comprehensive vetting process, which includes biometrics, should be a prerequisite before training any foreign military personnel. Sadly, we have a serious policy gap in this area, and as a result these kinds of biometrics-enabled background checks of the foreign military personnel we train are typically not performed.*

* After the initial drafting of this section, *The Washington Post* (November 28, 2014) reported that the DoD would be employing biometrics as part of a comprehensive screening program for Syrian rebel fighters who will receive military training. Sadly, this commonsense approach is described as being "unique to Syria," which indicates that, despite long-standing efforts by some in the biometrics community, there will still be no DoD policy mandating biometric screening before providing military training to foreign personnel.

## BIOMETRICS CAN HELP DETECT INSIDER THREATS

2011–2012 saw a significant increase in attacks by trusted, often uniformed, Afghans on U.S. Coalition allies. In many cases, these attacks were spur-of-the-moment events by Afghans upset about some actual or imagined personal slight or disgruntled about a less personal issue such as incidents of reported desecration of the Koran. However, in a number of instances such attacks were the work of local nationals acting on behalf of the insurgency. One way to help counter threats of the latter category is to use biometrics as part of a comprehensive insider threat detection program, which would include initial vetting of foreign military personnel that will have regular contact with our forces, as well as ongoing monitoring by counterintelligence personnel using a variety of technical means, including overt and covert biometric collection. According to an article in the January 2013 edition of the *Marine Corps Lessons Learned Newsletter*, Marines in Afghanistan used biometrics as part of the screening process for local Afghan security force members they were training (see Figure 5.3). These biometric

**Figure 5.3** A member of the Musa Qa'leh Police Advisor Team, Regimental Combat Team 6 (RCT-6), employs handheld interagency identity detection equipment (HIIDE) to record the biometrics of an Afghan Local Police (ALP) trainee at the Musa Qa'leh District Center in northern Helmand Province. Marines use the HIIDE to enter biometrics and other information on the trainees into the database, with one of the primary purposes being to help mitigate the insider threat. (Adapted from *Marine Corps Lessons Learned* (MCLL) *Newsletter*, Vol. 9/Issue 7, January 2013, p. 7.)

collections could result in matches to persons on the watchlist for immediate action by friendly forces or at least ensure that we have the biometrics in our database in the event that these trusted insiders are linked to future insurgent activities.

## BIOMETRICS FOR TACTICAL FORCE PROTECTION

Tactical forces conducting operations are responsible for providing their own security during movement and when halted. Tactical movements by larger forces, such as at the brigade level or higher, may include the employment of screening forces, such as scouts or cavalry units, to provide security to the front, rear, and flanks of a force in movement. While the United States did not conduct these kinds of large-scale operations for most of the past decade of combat (with the exception of the initial invasion of Iraq), we did conduct many operations at the battalion level and below, and the forces involved in these missions also required protection from surprise or attack. In an operation among a civilian population of uncertain loyalties, it is important that these screening elements, whether they are conducting patrols or establishing hasty checkpoints, are equipped with biometrics collection devices that have been uploaded with the current watchlist.

## SCENARIO: DEFENSIVE BIOMETRICS

These procedures provided immediate benefit, both in terms of the initial force protection impact and by fostering increased biometric collection, in order to help populate the local biometric database. Early in the operation, the Task Force Commander met with a senior police official in Mogadishu to discuss security and training arrangements, but the meeting was halted when the official was found to be on the DoD BEWL as a result of an earlier incident that occurred while he was working as a TCN on a Coalition base in Iraq.* The meeting continued after some moments of embarrassing discussion. In a potentially more serious incident, the fingerprints of a local businessman/powerbroker, who was going to be awarded a contract to provide external base and port security for U.S. forces in the Kismayo area, were matched to a set of latent prints taken off a cache of documents

* He had been fired from his job and barred from base access after being accused of stealing.

and currency recovered during an earlier raid on a suspected pirate facility. Needless to say, his company did not win the contract, and he was detained for extensive questioning before being transported to the capital and turned over to Somali national security officials.

The extensive biometric screening and overall collection requirements were viewed by Task Force commanders as a bit onerous at first, particularly early in the mission, when leadership engagements were limited and "contact" with the "enemy" was more often of a criminal nature than anything else. Still, the Task Force commander would grill his subordinate leaders during weekly meetings based upon the enrollment numbers reported by Major Johnson. Commanders, whose units produced low numbers of biometric collections, were "encouraged" to be more aggressive and more inventive in their biometrics activities.

Attitudes changed as the TF began to suffer casualties in small-arms and IED attacks and as raids and other offensive activity led to the collection of latent fingerprints from IED components and other material. When one of these prints matched the occupants of a local police vehicle, which was stopped at a hasty checkpoint during a humanitarian operation in Baidoa, the vehicle was immediately searched and found to contain a significant quantity of explosives rigged for remote detonation. Once word of this event got around, there were a great deal fewer complaints about the Task Force's biometrics force protection collection requirements.

# 6

# Biometrics Support to Operations across the Military Spectrum

Biometrics can help us locate, identify, target, and verify the identities of people we want to kill, capture or question. Biometrics can also reveal (or disprove) the identities of individuals who are trying to gain access to our personnel, facilities, supplies, and training in order to do us harm or for criminal mischief. But there are numerous other operational processes and activities, such as detainee control and management, legal actions, humanitarian operations, friendly personnel tracking and recovery, and medical support, to name just a few, that can be aided by the use of biometrics. All of these activities require the kind of accurate and timely identification, or identity verification, that biometrics can provide.

In this chapter, we will examine the following key concepts:

- Identification and identity verification via biometrics supports detention-related decision making and the entire detainee management process.
- Border control supported by biometrics can have a significant impact on the movement of enemy personnel and material.
- Biometrics support to the legal process became a powerful tool in countering the Iraqi insurgency and has been adopted by the Marines as a key component of their identity operations.

- Biometrics can support humanitarian operations by providing security and controlling access to resources.
- Biometrics could be a powerful tool to verify the identity of friendly forces, track their movements throughout the theater of operations, and enable rapid access to medical data.

## MANAGING DETAINEE PROCESSING AND HANDLING WITH BIOMETRICS

Determining who to detain, how to manage them, and who to release can have a major impact on the COIN fight. Employing the "vacuum cleaner" approach to detainment decision making, as we did initially in Iraq, can have a major impact, both on the attitude of the local population, and on the level of support from the international community—and even from our own civilian populace and political leadership. Moreover, no matter how well run, the typical detention facility is an ideal recruiting ground for insurgent and terrorist groups, so it is in our own best interest to keep the population of these facilities to the minimum possible, and to only detain those individuals who are really a threat to our forces, as opposed to those who just happen to have been in the area of an incident.* Equally important, is that we have the kind of information needed to keep the bad guys off the battlefield, to prosecute them if necessary (more on that later), and to ensure that when we do release someone, it is the right someone.

Determining who to detain sometimes begins with the intelligence and targeting processes described earlier, but more often than not, it begins with an encounter of some kind, with an unknown individual in the battlespace. For the first few years in Iraq, simply being a military-aged male or MAM and being in the wrong place at the wrong time (such as in the vicinity of an attack) could get you detained. This "detain them all and let God sort them out" approach, coupled with detentions based upon hearsay or spurious intelligence reporting (usually HUMINT), led to a rapid rise in the detainee population, overcrowding of detention

* See the comments in the Foreword from Major General (Retd.) Custer, regarding the impact that expanded use of biometrics could have had on our detention practices and the rise of the insurgency in Iraq.

**Figure 6.1** Secretary of Defense Donald H. Rumsfeld tours the notorious Abu Ghraib Detention Center on May 13, 2004. The report from the military investigation recommended the expanded use of biometrics for detainee management. (DoD released photo.)

facilities, and the all-too-often breakdown of control that resulted in the kinds of problems found at Abu Ghraib (Figure 6.1).*

The environment in Afghanistan was considerably different from that in Iraq in large part because we were operating in a country with a much greater sense of its own sovereignty (after the election of President Karzai, certainly) than was the case in Iraq until January 2005.† In Afghanistan there were strict rules as to how long you could detain an individual without a certain degree of proof that they were involved in insurgent activity, and oftentimes that proof rested upon tying an individual to an incident via biometrics. This made the collection of biometrics a key element of the detention process that began with the initial encounter with a suspected insurgent, terrorist, or their supporters. As long as the individual remained in U.S. custody, that initial biometric information could follow him/her throughout the detention "lifecycle," to include during transfer

* According to early BAT developer Anthony Iasso, whom I interviewed, one of the initial applications for the BAT system was detainee-management.

† The U.S.-led Coalition officially transferred sovereignty to the Iraqis on June 28, 2004, with the Iraqis forming an interim government under an appointed and interim President and Prime Minister. The first legislative elections were not held until January 2005.

between units or levels of detention, while being questioned or interrogated, or when being approved for release. This data could also be very useful in assisting in the recovery of escaped prisoners.*

The United States developed a biometrically-based system specifically designed to assist in tracking and management of detainees throughout their complete time in detention. This system, called the Detainee Management System (DMS), was based upon the same hardware as the BAT (Biometric Automated Toolset) and was designed to enroll and track detainees. Despite being similar in appearance and function to the BAT, the DMS software did not appear to be directly compatible with the BAT system used by forces in the field—meaning that the data exchange between the two separate systems required a resource-intensive manual process. At one point during my deployment, we received a request from the unit running the U.S. Theater Internment Facility (TIF) at Bagram Airbase to come reenroll all of their detainees into the BAT system so that they could determine if any were on the BEWL (Biometrics-Enabled Watchlist). The inability to share data quickly, and in an automated manner, was a serious gap, and one which prevented operational forces using the BAT from having immediate access to the detainee data, which could be critical to decision making during an operational encounter with a former detainee or, perhaps, one who had escaped custody. Despite the flaws of the system used in Iraq and Afghanistan, having a biometrics-based system like the DMS for detainee management is a critical component of any tactical detention program.†,‡

* The situation in Afghan prisons was VERY different than in the Coalition-run detention facilities, with the Afghans lacking any semblance of a prisoner management system, "biometrically-enabled" or otherwise. Many of those who were arrested remained imprisoned under horrible conditions until they either died, or had their release purchased by family members, or escaped. During my deployment, I had the chance to speak with members of a team sent to investigate the conditions in the Afghan and U.S. detention systems and to make recommendations for improvements. One of the basic problems they noted on the Afghan side was that there were individuals who had been paid to claim the identities of wanted criminals and to "do the time" for them.

† An alternative to developing and employing a system designed specifically for detainee management is simply to use whatever biometric system is employed by operational forces. While such a system might lack unique software and associated forms needed by the detainee-management process, it would at least ensure that detainee-related data could be rapidly exchanged with the systems in use by operational elements.

‡ Quoted text in the box ("Recommendations from the Taguba Report") is from Department of the Army Memorandum, Subject: "Certification (AR 15-6 Investigation of the 800th Military Police Brigade)," dated 4 June 2004.

## RECOMMENDATIONS FROM THE TAGUBA REPORT

In the wake of the Abu Ghraib crisis in Iraq, the U.S. Department of Defense created a commission to study the problems at the US detention facilities in Iraq and make recommendations regarding the culpability of key individuals, and to determine what policies and procedures should be enacted to ensure that this did not reoccur. The commission was led by a senior Army military police officer, Major General Antonio M. Taguba. The final report made a number of recommendations regarding biometrics use in support of detainee processing and management, including that "all units must be resourced and trained properly to use Biometrics Automated Toolset Systems (BATS) technology to facilitate detainee accountability and management in order to enable mission accomplishment. The use of this technology will enhance accountability procedures but not replace doctrinally proven techniques that must be reinforced." Later in the report it specifically calls for the use of the DRS and BATS to "facilitate real time updating when detainees are moved and or transferred from one location to another."

## BIOMETRICS AT THE BORDER

Most successful insurgencies have at least some measure of dependence upon support from outside the country in which they are operating. This has certainly been the case in both Iraq and Afghanistan. In Iraq, the flow of weapons and foreign fighters from Syria was a key source of strength for the Sunni insurgency, while Shiite groups received significant support, including weapons and training, from across the country's border with Iran. In Afghanistan, Taliban fighters flowed back and forth across the border with Pakistan, where much of the senior leadership of the group, as well as senior officials of the allied Haqqani network, found sanctuary. Interdicting, controlling, or simply monitoring the flow of personnel and supplies to an insurgency from neighboring countries is a key element of any successful COIN (counterinsurgency) campaign.

American forces in Iraq quickly established border checkpoints, often with biometrics support, in order to stem the flow of fighters and material into the country. These efforts continued through much of the occupation until border security was transferred to Iraqi control in June 2004.

The United States continued to provide support for Iraqi border forces, which included biometrics enrollment services provided via a contract supported by the BIMA (Biometrics Identity Management Agency). Other agencies provided similar capabilities in the effort to interdict material and manpower support coming out of Syria and Iran in support of Sunni insurgents and radical Shia groups.*

The situation was different in Afghanistan because U.S. Forces and our Coalition allies operated in a sovereign country, except for the immediate time after the fall of the Taliban government. Thus, the U.S. and its Coalition allies had much less influence over border control operations, particularly at the high-profile crossing sites such as the Torkham Gate border crossing point with Pakistan. Here, at the country's busiest crossing point, the U.S. military presence and our biometrics operations were minimized in order to not appear that we were undermining the Government of Afghanistan's sovereignty or complicating its critical and often contentious relationship with its neighbor.

One of the issues that I took on, during my time in Afghanistan, was to try getting support for the expansion of biometrics collections at Torkham. At the time, the United States was only able to perform minimal, and mostly voluntary, collections of a fraction of the foot traffic that crossed the border from Pakistan each day. This was due to a number of factors, including a lack of dedicated facilities for biometric collections, an absence of commercial electrical power, minimal force protection, and insufficient biometric collection and communications equipment.† These physical shortfalls were magnified by the lack of a formal policy agreement between the U.S./ISAF (International Security and Assistance

---

* My former organization, the BTF/BIMA, provided the funding for a number of years for a contract that supported biometric enrollments at key Iraqi Ports of Entry (PoEs), including a number of airports and border crossing sites. These activities were eventually transferred to Iraqi control.

† Thousands of Afghans cross the border through the Torkham Gate border site (*aka* Khyber Pass) on foot every day, presenting an ideal opportunity to collect biometrics and, possibly, interdict Afghan fighters and their support. Until the fall of 2009, ISAF biometrics operations consisted of a single team of collectors using the Handheld Interagency Identity Detection Equipment (HIIDE) device with no direct communications to the local BAT network or to the DoD biometrics database, which greatly hampered the transmission of new collections and the receipt of match-reporting and watchlist updates. Moreover, because U.S. forces stationed at the nearby FOB (Forward Operating Base) Torkham could only spare troops for force-protection support a few days a week, collection was limited to around six hours a day 3-4 times per week. The situation improved in late 2009–early 2010, with the establishment of improved facilities and expanded cooperation with local Afghan security forces.

**Figure 6.2** U.S. soldiers use HIIDE to collect biometrics at the Torkham Gate border crossing in Afghanistan. U.S. and ISAF forces failed to provide adequate biometrics support for border control for much of the war in Afghanistan and, thus, missed opportunities to interdict the flow of personnel and material supporting the insurgency.

Forces), the Government of Afghanistan and the Government of Pakistan, which would have allowed for more robust collection operations. The result was that we undoubtedly missed many opportunities to enroll, and possibly interdict, key persons of interest who crossed the border on a regular basis (Figure 6.2).*

While the situation on the border eventually improved, particularly with the addition of basic facilities and better protection, the establishment of an effective biometric collection capability at all of the key border

* A number of U.S. commanders, whose areas of responsibility included areas along the border, took it upon themselves to establish biometrically supported checkpoints near, but not usually at, key crossing points, in order to interdict insurgents and their support without appearing to be violating Afghan control of their own borders. In his previously cited draft article written for the Army's Center for Combined Army's Lessons Learned, Jerry Jackson noted that the U.S. Army's 173th Airborne Brigade effectively used HIIDE devices at checkpoints adjacent to the Afghanistan–Pakistan border to create "complex terrain" for insurgents operating in the area.

crossing points should have been a much higher priority to both the ISAF leadership and to the commanders in the field, than it appears to have been. Such a capability would have included sufficient collection equipment and personnel to allow for 24/7 operations, adequate force protection, and communications capabilities, to provide near real-time reach back to the ABIS database in the United States. The lesson here is that biometrics support to border control in a COIN fight cannot be an afterthought, but must be part of the overall campaign to isolate the insurgency from the people and its support, and to deny it sanctuary in neighboring countries. Providing the resources to accomplish this, in regards to both material and to policy, should be part of the theater biometrics campaign plan.

## BIOMETRICS AND THE LEGAL FIGHT

As the Iraqis established their own governance capability, including the creation of a functional justice system, it became more and more important for detainees who were suspected of having committed serious attacks to be tried in Iraqi criminal courts. While the new requirement to build court cases against the enemy was very frustrating for many in the U.S. military, it served a number of key purposes, not the least of which was to build up the host nation's security and legal capacity (a key tenet of COIN) and to provide more legitimacy to the Coalition's overall efforts. An important part of this effort in the early stages was to educate members of the Iraqi judicial system on the importance of forensic and biometric evidence. Prior to the destruction of the Hussein regime, the Iraqis had a legal system with somewhat of a western (French) basis—or at least as much as could be the case in a country under a dictatorship. Still, there were some elements of a traditional Shariah-based system, such as the preference for eyewitness accounts over more technical kinds of evidence. This latter aspect was particularly problematic, because we usually did not see insurgents planting their IEDs (Improvised Explosive Devices), and even if we did, it's questionable if the typical Iraqi judge would fully accept the eyewitness account of a U.S. soldier.

Fortunately, the United States was able to establish an effective training program for members of the Iraqi judiciary, which educated them on the collection and processing of forensic evidence, particularly in regards to the accuracy of fingerprinting and DNA-matching. The result of this training program was a gradual acceptance by the Iraqi legal system of the use of forensic evidence in court cases against insurgent or terrorist suspects, particularly when that evidence was supported by expert testimony from subject-matter experts. In fact, this process became so successful that the Marines in Fallujah set up an operational/legal process, which involved lawyers, military police, intelligence analysts, and forensics/biometric experts, working together to use "prosecution as a weapon system." Essentially, the entire operational process became, in effect, a legal process from the development of warrants, to the capture of the individual and collection of evidence, to the prosecution of these individuals in Iraqi courts. The success of this process was significant enough that it has been incorporated into Marine Corps doctrine and is part of the USMC (U.S. Marine Corps) Identity Operations program.*

## BIOMETRICS SUPPORT FOR HUMANITARIAN OPERATIONS

In a COIN fight, winning the support of the civilian populace, or at least neutralizing the influence of the insurgents, is a key objective. One of the ways this can be done is through the provision of humanitarian aid and support. We have previously noted that humanitarian missions provide excellent opportunities to collect biometrics and build up our database. But there are other reasons to employ biometrics in support of humanitarian operations, whether these are part of a COIN campaign or even if they are during separate, noncombat missions.

No matter the nature of the operation, security is always a consideration when providing humanitarian support. Being able to screen the local populace for members of terrorist or insurgent groups, or even for ordinary criminals, can make a big difference in securing the mission, protecting the friendly forces executing the missions, and preventing

* Using the legal process as a counterinsurgency weapon has been much slower to develop in Afghanistan than it was in Iraq, mainly due to the country's lack of a functioning legal system or even rudimentary technical capabilities for law enforcement. In 2009, the United States was preparing to provide the Afghan Ministry of the Interior (MoI) with a forensics lab that could be used to train Afghan law enforcement personnel and eventually be transferred to them to form the basis for a national forensics program. I visited the existing MoI "lab" and saw that the Afghan's forensics capabilities were so rudimentary as to essentially be nonexistent, including a lack of such basic supplies as latex gloves. My understanding is that the subsequent ISAF effort to help build an Afghan forensics capability has not met with much success.

the humanitarian resources themselves from ending up in the hands of insurgents or criminals. Biometrics can also help to regulate the provision of resources, whether they are food, school supplies, building materials, or medicines, from being unevenly distributed, which could benefit one group at the expense of another or which could be sold on the blackmarket by profiteers. In the case of medicines such as inoculations, this ability to monitor and track distribution may have an important safety impact as well.*

I previously noted that collecting biometrics during humanitarian missions is a good way to help build your database, but this is more likely to be the case when such missions occur as part of a combat operation. When humanitarian missions are undertaken in a noncombat environment, it may not be possible or politically feasible to use the data collected for other purposes. This may especially be the case when such missions fall under the auspices of an international body such as the United Nations. In such cases, biometric collections are likely to be stored and used locally for the duration of the mission only. When the mission is concluded, such data could be deleted or transferred to the control of the host nation authorities (see Figure 6.3).†

## BIOMETRICS FOR FRIENDLY-FORCE IDENTITY VERIFICATION AND TRACKING

The last two battlefield biometric applications that I am going to discuss, are focused on the health and welfare of our own soldiers, which is a usage that the United States has been hesitant to pursue due to privacy concerns and the absence of well-defined requirements. The first application is the employment of biometrics for personnel accountability and recovery. We currently have numerous ways of tracking our personnel during the deployment process through the use of such legacy methods as

* According to an article posted (October 6, 2014) on the Planet Biometrics website, a computer science professor at Michigan State University has developed a fingerprint-based system to track which vaccines children have been given. The system is being targeted specifically at developing nations.

† The UN High Commissioner for Refugees (UNHCR) has been testing the use of biometrics to manage refugee populations in its refugee operations for a number of years. In 2013, the office issued a request for proposals for a biometric identity management system to register and verify the identities of refugees and regulate access to UNHCR-provided resources.

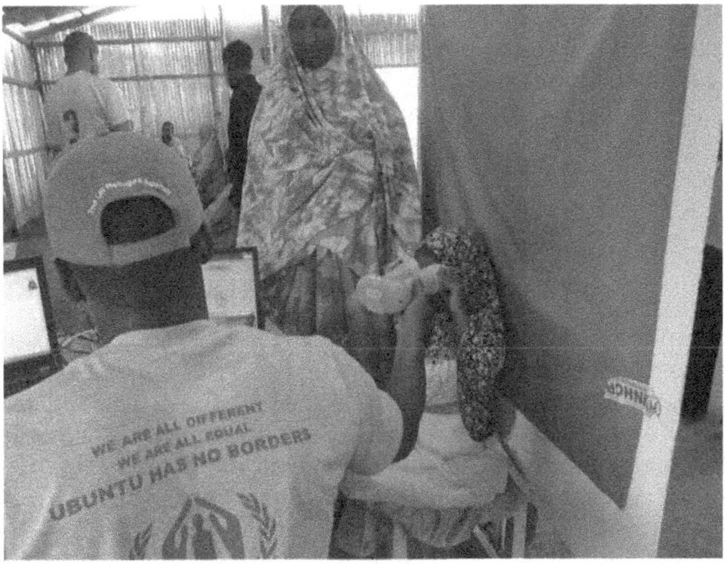


**Figure 6.3** UNHCR biometrics collection at a Malawi refugee camp.

paper manifests and hard-copy logs. Unfortunately, the data cannot generally be shared across various applications. Employing a biometric-based system could tie the tracking data to the associated biometric signature, which could serve as the unique identifier associating the individual to the data in the central database. The same biometric data and tracking system could be used throughout the individual's time in the combat theater, to include when he or she departed from a base to conduct a patrol or other combat activity. Should an individual go missing during an operation, the same biometric data could be used to verify his or her identity once the individual (or his/her remains) has been located. This would be a vast improvement over the current system of providing a DNA sample (*aka* "blood chit") in the U.S. prior to deployment and would enable us to have a true end-to-end biometric-based personnel tracking system.

Although we have successfully digitized our medical files and made the data potentially available, we cannot link that information definitively to a soldier who is wounded and cannot provide any other means of identity verification, such as the age-old dog tag or an ID card. The situation is so pathetic that some combat troops in Afghanistan and Iraq adopted the practice of tattooing their blood type on their bodies, in case they became wounded and could not communicate. Fortunately, the technology exists today to create a system that would quickly and securely connect an individual to his/her medical information using biometrics.

## SCENARIO: BIOMETRICS FOR DETAINEE MANAGEMENT AND BORDER CONTROL IN OPERATION GORDON

By late spring 2016, military operations by the Task Force, as well as more aggressive actions by the Somali national security forces, led to a major increase in the number of detainees. Most of those detained were not assessed as being directly associated with terrorist groups considered to be Al Qaeda "franchises" or to be involved in attacks on the Coalition allies. By previous agreement, most detainees were turned over to the Somali government for holding and eventual legal processing. Despite this, the number of detainees being held by the Coalition soon exceeded the capacity of the coalition facility at the international airport. Around the same time, the Somalis began complaining that the influx of detainees was straining their own prison facility capabilities as well as mixing suspected dangerous militants and terrorists with the general criminal population. At a meeting in mid-May, the Coalition leaders agreed to establish a combined Coalition/Somali military detention/processing facility at the Mogadishu Soccer Stadium.

Now, the Coalition staff had to figure out how to do it. The Coalition Commander attended the initial planning meeting, at which he declared: "I'm not going to have any goddamn Abu Ghraibs on my watch. We are going to do this right and by the book." Unfortunately, the book on combined detainee operations in a barely Third World environment had not yet been written, so the staff focused on two key issues: identifying and managing the detainee population (and in particular how to keep the hardcore Islamist leaders away from the low-level militant foot soldiers and opportunists), and creating a process that could eventually be maintained by the Somalis. Someone at the meeting suggested using biometrics as a way to aid in prisoner management, so Major Johnson was soon brought into the discussions. Although he was still in college when the Abu Ghraib crisis occurred, he recalled reading in a recently published book on biometrics that the Army had created a Detainee Management System, which it used at Abu Ghraib and other detention facilities in Iraq and later on in Afghanistan. He contacted the AFRICOM IDRes (the U.S. Africa Command's Identity Resolution) element in Djibouti and asked for assistance. None of them had direct knowledge of the system but they had the same book and noted that the DMS had been developed by army intelligence personnel at the Language Technology Office (LTO) in Fort Huachuca, Arizona.

The Army G2 assisted AFRICOM in contacting the LTO. Although the original DMS had never been fielded as an enduring program, they still had the original software and, more importantly, some additional BAT kits for which it had been designed. Since the system was going to be operated by Somalis, they integrated the original DMS capabilities into the Multilingual Automated Registration System (MARS), which would allow the Somalis to operate an Arabic language version of the system. The LTO was able to create an updated version of MARS/DMS, upload it into the available BATs, and send them to the Task Force within a matter of weeks.

Once the systems were on hand and the locally hired enrollers were trained, the Combined Detainee Processing Center (CDPC) was open for business.* The first effort was to perform full enrollments and to badge all current detainees. The data from these enrollments was used to create new BAT records and to provide additional information, including better quality biometrics, for existing records. The newly captured, higher-quality images resulted in a number of new identifications. One individual who had been detained by U.S. forces during the operations in Baraawe was not just a local tribesman guarding an IED production site, as he had been identified at the time, but was in fact an expert IED-maker, whose fingerprints had been found on quite a few devices captured in western Iraq in 2007. Further, a number of detainees originally assessed by the Somalis as being low-level militants were in fact key Al Shabaab figures, including one who turned out to be a major watchlisted terrorist. This information helped ensure a proper segregation of detainees, which aided in keeping the population relatively calm and under control.

The BAT badge and Pier device combination also aided in managing the population and was used at all roll calls, during detainee movements/transfers, and for spot checks. Since the badges had a picture, detainees originally thought they could exchange them among those that looked similar. However, this practice ceased once they realized that the

* During their training, the trainees enrolled themselves, which resulted in a number of them being detained when their fingerprints matched against those in the ABIS.

**Figure 6.4** The U.S. Department of State has provided the PISCES border control system to select countries to help deter the crossborder movement of terrorists.

iris system was not fooled, and once the establishment of policies was designed to discourage such practices. The detention facility was also equipped with a network of Radio-frequency Identification (RFID) readers, which could read the badges from a distance, making it possible to do automated queries of detainee locations at various parts of the day, as well as to determine which detainees were likely meeting with one another. This allowed CDPC officials to interrupt planning for a number of potential detainee disruptions and at least one planned escape attempt.

Having established successful biometric capabilities inside the country, Major Johnson next looked at how the Task Force could use biometrics to interdict crossborder movement of militants and their supplies. The successful tactical interdiction efforts during the Baraawe raid were followed by efforts to establish permanent biometrics collections sites near key border crossing points throughout the country (Figure 6.4).* Inside the country, the Task Force essentially created a border control force

* PISCES stands for Personal Identification Secure Comparison and Evaluation System. The program is managed by the U.S. State Department and is offered to selected countries which lack effective border-control capabilities but which are assessed to be key transit points for transnational terrorists. According to Wikipedia, the system includes biometric collection of facial and fingerprint images, but initial deployments only included the ability to identify individuals using biographical data. It is unclear if all current PISCES systems have biometric capabilities. The Wiki page identifies Kenya as one of the countries where PISCES is planned to be deployed.

for the Somali Government, which it trained and supplied with biometrics systems for both fixed and mobile collection. Although this overall capability did achieve a number of successful interdictions and identifications of suspected militants (as well as causing some to alter their movement patterns to avoid collection), the challenges of data movement and shortage of trained collectors often hampered biometrics border control efforts.

# 7

# What's Next for Military (and Other) Biometrics Operations?

To this point in the book, I've largely focused on how to improve and expand the use of biometrics within the confines of current intelligence, offensive, defensive, and supporting applications. In this chapter, I will focus on some ways in which biometrics could be used on the battlefield beyond just finding bad guys and defending ourselves from them. I'm also going to look a bit into the future at how technical developments may affect the military use of biometric technologies.

The title of this chapter asks the question, "What's next" for biometrics? We might better ask: Is there anything next? Will the United States or other countries that have developed military biometrics capabilities over the past decade continue to pursue more sophisticated technologies that can support an even greater array of military tasks, or will spending on biometrics be seen as a unnecessary expense in an increasingly fiscally constrained postwar environment? As far as the U.S. military is concerned, expanding or even maintaining the capabilities we have acquired will require some trade-offs with more traditional capabilities that may not be palatable. This situation is complicated by the fact that biometrics does not fit cleanly into any one military capability area and, thus, it is difficult to fund under the budgeting process used by the military services. On the other hand, employment of identification technologies by governments, for law enforcement and border control/homeland security, and by the private sector (particularly overseas) has seen significant growth, so it stands to reason that militaries will adopt many of these same capabilities over time. It may also be that countries other than the United States will take the lead in employing biometrics within their militaries, both because of the increased use in their civil commercial sectors, and because some countries (e.g., Pakistan, Egypt, China, Philippines, Nigeria), will continue to struggle with active terrorist/insurgent threats in which biometrics can play a critical role in successfully combating.

Specifically, Chapter 7 will focus on the following key concepts:

- Biometrics will become increasingly important for friendly ("Blue") force applications, including personnel management/ accountability, security, and access control.
- Technologies for stand-off and mobile collection, particularly those based upon facial recognition, will improve and become more operationally useful.
- There will be improved forensics applications of biometrics, especially rapid DNA processing and matching and automated latent print matching.
- The future will see "biometrics ubiquity," including biometrics embedded in targeting sensors and perhaps in sensors for the terminal guidance of munitions.
- Biometrics may be used to supplement or replace current means of encrypting data or voice communications.
- Other USG (U.S. Government) elements have similar needs to the military for identification and identity verification and should develop their own biometrics capabilities:
  - U.S. State Department: Diplomatic security and support for nontraditional diplomacy
  - U.S. Secret Service: Threat identification and overseas presidential security

## INCREASING FOCUS ON "BLUE FORCE" CAPABILITIES

If we assume that there will continue to be military use of biometrics and continued development of military-related biometrics capabilities, what might this usage and development look like? Initially, I believe there will be a much greater use of biometrics for friendly personnel management, security, and access control. This is what my former organization used to call "Blue Force Biometrics" and it involves the incorporation of biometrics and biometrics identity management capabilities into a whole host of applications, some of which I described in the previous chapter (e.g., personnel tracking and recovery and medical). The use of biometrics will become increasingly common across all areas that require individual identification or identity verification, including: access to computer networks, facilities, and resources (including weapons and munitions); access to individual personnel and medical records; financial transactions (both individual pay and "corporate" transactions, such as contracts); and for continuous security vetting of personnel. These biometric enhancements will be made in part because they mirror those taking place across the civil sector, but also because of the general move towards the interconnectedness of identity data across multiple applications.

## IMPROVEMENT IN STANDOFF AND MOBILE COLLECTION

From the perspective of combat operations, there will be a move towards the fielding of biometric collection systems that provide better standoff distance between sensor and target, which will make them more suitable for protecting forces in the field. Most of this employment will be based upon facial recognition, which has already experienced rapid growth and improvement in accuracy from greater ranges, particularly when supported by matching systems that allow for "off angle" facial images to be matched using 3D modeling. Capturing and matching facial images while on the move, or from moving targets (via video to still image or video to video matching), will also become increasingly viable at least for threat warning or intelligence purposes. Capturing and matching iris images from a distance, or while on the move, may also see increased usage, but more likely for standoff identification/verification for access control than in support of troops in field operations. Even if the accuracy of these capabilities is not initially sufficient for fully automated (*aka* "Lights Outs") identification or verification, they may still be useful when fused with other capabilities, such as some type of automated weapons detection system or when used in conjunction with data from intelligence sources.

## IMPROVED FORENSICS CAPABILITIES

In the forensics area, rapid and fully automated DNA processing and matching capabilities, which can be deployed in the forward area, will see increased use. There is a great deal of research and development being done in this area for both the law enforcement and military applications,

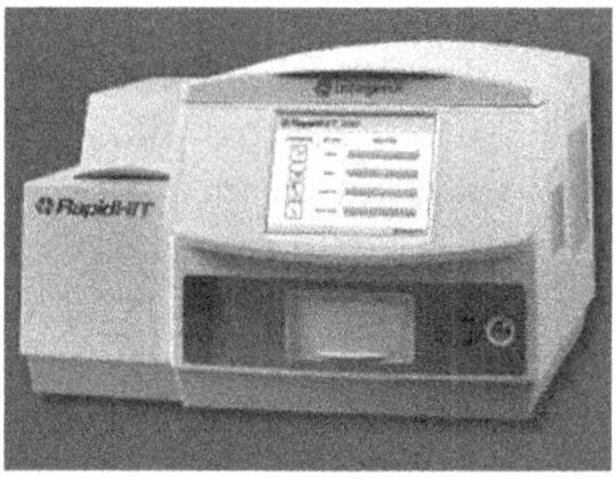

**Figure 7.1** The RapidHIT® system by IntegenX distributed by MorphoTrust USA. Rapid DNA processing and matching systems will make DNA much more useful for combat identification.

and this will eventually lead to systems that will allow a common soldier or policemen to extract a DNA sample from the scene of a crime or attack, or from a suspect, and make a match with enough accuracy and enough speed to support a decision to arrest or detain a subject (see Figure 7.1).*

The ability to digitally collect fingerprints, and perhaps even do matching against live prints or latent prints stored on a collection device, will also become viable, and this will have a major impact on the ability to quickly identify individuals involved in insurgent or terrorist activity, particularly those who support or conduct IED (Improvised Explosive Device) attacks. The current latent print process will be discussed in more detail in Appendix C, but suffice it to say that the need for specialized training and equipment for the extraction and processing of latent prints and the inability of the most commonly used biometric collection systems to perform automated matching of latent prints seriously hampers their use for time-sensitive identification; however, more advanced collection systems and matching algorithms will likely correct these deficiencies over time.†

* I attended the Global Identity Summit in September 2014 and viewed a presentation of IntegenX's rapid DNA processing and matching system which is distributed by MorphoTrust USA. This version, which is similar to others being developed, offers a 90-minute response from submission of sample to match against an existing/stored profile.

† A number of vendors, such as Booze Allen Hamilton, with its newly announced "Vampire" tactical forensics device, claim that recently developed collection systems are capable of digital latent print collection and matching. Given the current state of research into the subject of automated latent print matching, I would say that I am more than a bit skeptical about BAH's claims. Despite this skepticism, I describe a how a force might use a tactical forensics collection and matching system in the scenario at the end of Chapter 4. So while I believe such a capability is needed and coming to a battlefield in the future, I just do not believe it's here yet.

While collection systems seem to attract the most interest from the R&D (research and development) community, there will also be improvements on the database side, the most significant of which will be automated matching for latent prints. The current latent matching process used by the Department of Defense (and law enforcement) requires a manual comparison of latent print matches for at least the top candidates produced by the automated system. This process delays the match return by a minimum of a couple of hours (or oftentimes more) dependent upon who the submitter is and the communications links between them and the U.S. DoD biometrics database (i.e., ABIS).* The National Institute for Standards and Technology has been studying this issue for some time and is evaluating the accuracy of various latent print matching systems. Accuracy appears to be approaching the level that may be sufficient for military operational applications if not for legal prosecution. I will discuss this more in Appendix C.

## BIOMETRICS UBIQUITY

Beyond the applications I describe above, I believe that the future for military biometrics will be the development of a comprehensive tactical identity management system, which will integrate biometrics with a full suite of sensors that are integrated into the soldier's personal equipment and weapons systems. At the individual level, this "every soldier a *biometric* sensor"† approach will be based upon what a recent government panel described as "cheap and ubiquitous biometrics."‡ This approach will see the incorporation of biometrics as a system of systems that will aid in the tracking and management of individual personnel, provide for the monitoring of current medical conditions and for access to historical medical data, allow for security and access control (no more passwords), support communications security (no more need for call signs), aid in intelligence collection, and provide target identification/verification. Soldiers' weapons may be linked to their

* I have always believed that mastering the latent print problem for the military requires not only more advanced technology, but also an examination of the current practices, which, I believe, are too wedded to a law enforcement style process, where a higher degree of certainty is required than may be necessary for many military battlefield identification applications.

† Similar to Army intelligence's longstanding concept of providing technology to make "every soldier a sensor."

‡ This statement comes from an article posted on the FierceHomelandSecurity website about the 2013 annual leadership meeting of the American Council for Technology (ACT)–Industry Advisory Council (IAC) held in Williamsburg, VA.

biometrics, as well to provide an extra layer of security to prevent stolen or captured weapons from being sold or used by an enemy.

I also see an increased role in biometrics, both as part of the target development process and perhaps integrated with target acquisition systems, or even within terminal guidance systems, for individual munitions.* Perhaps the scope on a sniper rifle could have an integrated facial recognition capability for improved targeting? Back when I started as an intelligence officer, they used to say that our imagery satellites allowed us to "count the dimples on a golf ball." I don't know if that was actually the case then, or if it is now, but I do believe that if you can capture an image of a person's face with enough clarity, no matter is if it is from 100 feet or 100 miles, you can potentially perform facial recognition. It may be possible, sooner rather than later, to accurately identify and track individuals in this way, which would both vastly improve our intelligence collection, and make it far more likely that we are taking kinetic action against the real target and not just someone who happens to be in the wrong place at the wrong time. As we transition out of the direct fighting of insurgents and terrorists in Afghanistan and focus even more on taking the fight worldwide, I believe that there will be even more emphasis on accuracy in targeting and attacking bad guys, particularly when those attacks occur inside sovereign nations. Biometrics can provide the increased accuracy that will be required in this new operational environment.

## BIOMETRICS-BASED ENCRYPTION

At the risk of getting well beyond my limited technical skillset, I am going to make one final suggestion about a future military use for biometrics, and that is to support communications security. Biometric-based encryption could involve using an individual's unique biometrics characteristics to generate a separately produced encryption algorithm. For example, placing a finger on the fingerprint sensor embedded in the handset of a tactical radio would authenticate the user to the communications system and cause it to encrypt the communications using a set of previously developed algorithms. Alternately, the data in the biometric template itself could be used to generate a new and unique algorithm to encrypt the communications. This may not be as crazy as it sounds—there has

* I used to joke about developing a cruise missile or a "really smart" bomb that could be programed with the facial image or iris scan of an individual target, but perhaps this application may not really be so farfetched.

been academic research into this application of biometrics going back at least as far as 2005.* Biometric encryption could be used to supplement or replace current communications system-based encryption and could also have the advantage of identifying the specific/individual speaker in a tactical communication, without the need for a call sign or other identifier.

## HOW CAN BIOMETRICS BE USED IN NONMILITARY "OPERATIONS"?

This book was intended to focus on military uses of biometrics, but there are obviously many other government functions beyond the military that have similar needs to accurately identify individuals for both defensive and offensive missions. In the many biometrics and related meetings and forums I have attended over the years, I have met representatives from many USG agencies that are involved with the use of biometrics capabilities to varying degrees; however, two organizations have stood out by their absence at these forums: the U.S. State Department, and the U.S. Secret Service. In over seven years of attending forums, meetings, and discussions with representatives from across the U.S. government, I have only rarely seen a representative from the State Department participating.† I have never seen anyone from the Secret Service at any of these venues.

## BIOMETRICALLY ENABLED DIPLOMACY AND DIPLOMATIC SECURITY

Soon after the first reports of the attack on the U.S. Consulate in Benghazi (Figure 7.2), I became convinced that the U.S. State Department had an identification problem. It appears from descriptions in the media that U.S. diplomatic personnel in Libya lacked the ability to really know the true

* The University of Cambridge's Computer Laboratory published a Technical Report in July 2005 titled: "Combining cryptography with biometrics effectively." The paper specifically looked at deriving a biometric key from iris codes. An abstract published in July 2014 by IEEE titled: "Biometric Inspired Multimedia Encryption Based on Dual Parameter Fractional Fourier Transform" indicates research is continuing into this rather esoteric topic.

† I finally met a State Department rep for biometrics at the Biometrics Big Data Symposium held in Reston, VA, in June of 2014, after I wrote the original version of this section. Shortly thereafter, the Department issued a Request for Information regarding the use of biometrics for overseas facility security.

**Figure 7.2** Montage of publicly released photos of the aftermath of the Benghazi attack. The DoS has been very slow to adopt biometrics for security of its overseas facilities.

or full identities of representatives from the various militias or opposition groups with whom they were meeting, or in some cases, who they were employing. One "friendly" militia member was quoted in *The Washington Post* after the attack, as saying, "they didn't know an enemy from a friend." As I thought about this incident, as well as of the larger challenges that the Department has with the kinds of "nontraditional" diplomatic engagements common in places like Libya and Syria, it struck me that the State Department's identity needs to mirror those of the U.S. military in many ways. Like the military, the Department needs to protect its personnel and resources against threats, particularly from people who want access to its facilities, those who they will work for them, or people and companies from whom they will purchase services. Like the military, it also needs to have the ability to identify its "targets," to ensure that its diplomatic operations are directed at the right people. And, when conducting diplomatic operations, our officials in our embassies need the ability to verify the identities of those with whom they are engaging, particularly when those individuals do not possess strong and verifiable official credentials.*

It is a bit ironic that the State Department is just now looking at incorporating an internally focused biometrics capability when it is one of the most prolific direct collectors of identity data on foreign persons, including biometrics, in the U.S. Government. According to publicly available

* Members of nongovernmental organizations, political opposition groups, and militia groups, with whom our embassies engage, are not usually officials of the countries in which they operate, and thus have little to no official vetting.

information, State's Bureau of Consular Affairs processed over 11 million nonimmigrant visas in FY 2012. The standard application form, the DS-160, requires a great deal of biographical and associated information, including date and place of birth, aliases, current place of residence, family members' names, and contacts in the United States. In addition, all applicants are required to submit a facial photo, and many, if not most of those, will be required to have their fingerprints taken and then verified during the visa interview process.* This data is stored in State's Consolidated Consular Database (CCD) which, as of 2012, held over 151 million immigrant and nonimmigrant visa records.† The Department also maintains its own facial recognition capability at the Kentucky Consular Center, including both an automated system for facial image comparison, as well as facial recognition specialists who manually review the automated results when needed.‡ Thus, the U.S. State Department is one of the largest holders and users of biometrics in the United States Government.

The collected identity data is used by the Department to help it determine whether or not to approve visa applications. It is assisted in this effort by submitting the fingerprints of visa applicants to the FBI, DHS and DoD to be run through their biometric databases to determine if there is derogatory law enforcement or national security information on the applicants. However, beyond the visa approval process, it does not appear that the Department's considerable biometrics capability is employed to support its own security or operational needs. For example, even though biometrics are collected from every visa applicant, biometric systems are not used as part of access control to U.S. diplomatic facilities abroad, with the exception of the U.S. embassy in Iraq. In addition, though our overseas facilities are protected against attack in various ways, including the use of reinforced building materials and the employment of standoff distance from potential areas of attack, there is apparently no requirement to employ biometrics for standoff threat detection.§ Finally, although the Department

* Applicants from select "Visa Waiver" countries are not required to submit fingerprints as part of the visa process. However, they do have a requirement to submit biographical data and fingerprints under the Department of Homeland Security's Electronic System for Travel Authorization program.

† Current figures are not available, but as of 2009, there were over 75 million facial photos in the CCD.

‡ The facial photos are used to insure that individual applicants have not previously applied for a visa under a different name.

§ Interestingly, a short assessment published by the RAND Corporation after the Benghazi attack did not include biometrics among the technologies recommended to improve diplomatic facility security and protection.

has a significant, and perhaps growing, mission to engage with nonofficial foreign personnel, including members of political opposition groups and militias, there does not appear to be an effort to more accurately identify and vet these individuals.*

If the State Department were to create a holistic biometric capability, how might it be designed? First, the Department will need to procure its own automated multimodal biometric database/matching system, similar to the DoD ABIS, DHS Ident, or the FBI's New Generation Identification system. Alternatively, the Department might be able to work out an arrangement with DHS or FBI to have them perform their biometric data storage matching and operational support functions. The Department would also need to purchase a system for multimodel biometrics enrollment and verification, and immediately deploy it to its most vulnerable facilities to support local access control and security. Policies will need to be created with relevant host nations regarding data sharing (if any) as well as policies for collecting biometrics from "official" personnel or senior host nation officials. Direct biometrics collections for access to U.S. diplomatic facilities would need to be supplemented by a standoff facial recognition capability to identify potential threats to the most dangerous and vulnerable posts. Embassy or consulate officials should also have access to a handheld biometric collection capability to help them identify new or previously unvetted or nonofficial contacts, and to verify the identities of individuals who may have been the targets of previous diplomatic engagements, particularly if these occurred over significant spans of time, or were initiated in another location. Similar efforts would be taken to identify and vet those persons and organizations receiving U.S.-provided support, such as military or security force training or other State Department-administered aid.

As with the military applications of biometrics, the rapid movement of the biometric data between the various biometric-supported functions and between locations will be as critical to the State Department's biometric identification process as it is to the military's. Biometric enrollments must be shared with all local embassy elements (such as the Regional Security Office and the Consulate office), with all facilities in the region, and with the owners of appropriate database or databases in the United States.

* Such a capability would employ biometrics supported by a robust "identity intelligence" effort to help ensure we are engaging with the right people and not dealing with, or providing support for, individuals with ties to terrorist groups or criminal organizations, or who might be human rights violators.

A biometric watchlist should be developed at the local, regional, or national level to ensure that individuals previously identified and assessed as being potential threats are denied access to any U.S. diplomatic facility and are prevented from direct contact with U.S. personnel. For those persons who are not on a watchlist, the biometric database may include information that could be used to make immediate decisions on whether to grant them access to a diplomatic facility, to begin processing their visa request, or to allow them to have other contact with embassy personnel.*

Data collected by the Department itself, or acquired from other partner agencies, could also support a State Department identity intelligence (I2) capability. State's I2 effort would support a wide range of applications, including helping to identify individuals suspected of conducting surveillance of U.S. posts or personnel. I2 could also support the Department's diplomacy efforts by helping to identify and provide additional data on individuals who may not have full (or any) diplomatic credentials. The same capability could help determine who the key personnel are within a nongovernmental organization, including opposition and militia groups, so that we focus our engagements on the right people and avoid those individuals who could present a security threat and/or could lead to a potential diplomatic embarrassment. The following scenario shows how using biometrics could support U.S. diplomatic efforts.

## US STATE DEPARTMENT BIOMETRIC SCENARIO—NO MORE BENGHAZIS: BIOMETRICS SUPPORT TO DIPLOMACY AND DIPLOMATIC SECURITY

On August 1, 2015 Syrian President Bashar al-Asad was assassinated by dissident members of his military while visiting Syrian forces during the country's Armed Forces Day. His death led to a rapid dissolution of the Syrian regime and subsequent occupation of Damascus by moderate forces under the Syrian Free Army. Shortly after, the Syrian National Council announced the formation of an interim government. The U.S. quickly recognized the new government and vowed to immediately reopen its embassy in the chaotic capital along with deploying an acting ambassador and consulate staff. Immediate security for the facility and

* For instance, an individual who has been previously enrolled anywhere in the world would have biographical data on file that could reveal inconsistencies in their application for a visa or in their proposal to provide contracted support services to an embassy.

embassy officials would be provided by a contingent of U.S. Marines and, for the first time, a small team of biometrics technicians from the State Department's newly established Biometrics Identity Verification Program (BIVP). BIVP personnel consisted of biometrics enrollers and communications technicians equipped with the Program's interim collection system of excess DoD Biometrics Automated Toolsets (BATs) and Handheld Interagency Identification Equipment (HIIDE) devices. The BAT systems were used to screen all non-U.S. visitors to the embassy compound, who did not possess verifiable, official government credentials, and this included all National Council members. The systems were also used to screen local national hires, particularly members of a local "friendly" militia, which had been contracted to provide external security for the embassy compound. The local embassy Regional Security Officer insisted that HIIDE devices also be issued to the security details that accompanied embassy officials on meetings with members of the interim government and other "nongovernmental" organizations and that screening of these local contacts be performed before any substantive discussions occurred.

The BIVP also deployed a newly developed long-range facial recognition capability, the Securics FIINDER system (see Figure 7.3),* which was being operationally tested to see if it met the Department of State

**Figure 7.3** Long-range facial recognition capabilities, such as this Securics FIINDER system, were acquired by the DoS to provide enhanced security for its most vulnerable overseas facilities.

* The FIINDER system was developed by Securics, Inc. from Colorado Springs which recently went out of business. However, there are a number of other companies that are developing or have developed the capability to perform long-range facial recognition.

(DoS) requirement for standoff security for selected overseas facilities. The FIINDER would initially be set up on the roof of the U.S. Embassy in Damascus, but could also be deployed to future consulate locations in other Syrian cities such as Aleppo. Facial images of suspicious individuals captured by the system would be matched against previously collected images as well as sent via satellite communications to be processed and matched against the huge State Department facial image repository by facial recognition experts at the Kentucky Consular Center (KCC) in Lexington.

The watchlist was also provided to other DoS facilities in the region, including the U.S. Embassy in Amman, Jordan, where an individual who claimed to be a Syrian applying for a U.S. nonimmigrant visa, was revealed to be an Iraqi member of the radical Islamic group, the Islamic State in Iraq and the Levant (ISIL). In another incident, a HIIDE collection from an individual representing a Syrian nongovernmental organization (NGO) seeking U.S. funding did not immediately match against the watchlist. But when his fingerprints were transmitted back to the United States and matched against various biometric databases, he was identified as being the same individual whose visa application had been denied three years earlier because of suspected ties to Syrian intelligence. The embassy quickly broke contact with the NGO he represented.

A short while later, a series of suspicious surveillance events at the embassy were captured by the FIINDER system, which indicated that they were all conducted by the same individuals, but they could not be further identified. The images were transmitted back to the KCC, where they were eventually matched to earlier photos taken of an individual identified by the newly established Identity Intelligence Division of the State Bureau of Intelligence and Research, as the Chief of Security for the Syrian Free Army. A quick phone call confirmed that he had been reviewing the external security arrangements being provided for the embassy compound.

This scenario shows only a snapshot of how the U.S. State Department could employ biometrics and related capabilities, such as Identity Intelligence, to better protect its people and to improve the Department's overseas operations. As I stated earlier, the Department's needs in protecting its people and facilities and in identifying its diplomatic "targets" are very similar to those of the U.S. military. The technologies being used here are either being employed today (BATs/HIIDEs) or likely will be in the near future (i.e., standoff facial recognition). More importantly, the State Department already has a vast amount of experience in collecting and matching biometric signatures, as well as its own useful sources of biometric data. What is still needed, though, is for the Department to develop a strategy and secure the funding to fully integrate identity capabilities into all the nation's overseas diplomatic operations.

## WHY NOT USE BIOMETRICS TO PROTECT OUR GOVERNMENT'S MOST VALUABLE ASSET?

Biometrics has proven its value many times over in force-protection and personnel-vetting roles. Technical developments in standoff threat detection have the potential to greatly extend the distance at which we can detect, classify, and identify potential threats, particularly when integrating a biometrics with a system that may be able to determine intent.* So you might find it strange, as I do, that one organization which has not shown much of an interest in biometrics is the United States Secret Service (USSS). In over five years of direct involvement with DoD's biometrics programs I never encountered an individual representing the Secret Service at any biometrics-related meeting, conference or forum. A couple of years ago, I mentioned that observation to a neighbor of mine who is a career agent, and he said that he was not aware of any significant interest in developing a biometrics capability within his organization.†

One way to develop a case for the use of biometrics by the Secret Service is to examine a scenario where such a capability could have been useful. Fortunately for me, such a scenario developed just as I began to write this portion of my book and involves an incident that occurred during President Obama's December 2013 visit to South Africa, following the death of former South African President Nelson Mandela. During the memorial service at which the President spoke, he was joined on the stage by a man who was ostensibly serving as a sign language interpreter. Soon after that event, however, it was widely revealed in the media that this

* It might be possible to employ a biometric identification capability based on facial recognition with a biometric system that focuses on a behavioral characteristic, such as gait, to both identify a potential threat and determine the individual's intent. For example, a change in an individual's gait from that recorded previously might indicate the individual has a hidden weapon or is wearing a suicide vest.

† I have also tried to search the internet for "biometrics" and "Secret Service" thinking that I might find an example of some kind of contracting action, but all I have been able to uncover is a reference to the effort to hire a latent print examiner for the organization's forensics department.

**Figure 7.4** President Obama and the fake South African sign-language interpreter. This December 2013 incident highlights the need for a Secret Service biometrics identification program. (Officially released photo from whitehouse.gov.)

individual was actually an imposter who was not only mentally unstable but who had been previously charged with murder in South Africa. An article in *The Washington Post* described how the individual "faked his credentials," despite the South African government's previous pledge to conduct "all necessary" background checks on personnel involved in the visit (Figure 7.4).*

This embarrassing incident is an excellent example of why the Secret Service needs a biometrics program. In order to be fully effective, such a program would incorporate both mobile and static biometrics collection and matching capabilities (including a standoff capability and the ability to match collections immediately against a specially tailored watchlist), and the ability to rapidly transmit and match new collections against data in relevant U.S. databases and to receive timely match responses. One of the more challenging and politically sensitive aspects of a Secret Service biometrics program would be the development of biometric collection

* *The Washington Post* online, "Signer highlights U.S. security uncertainties abroad," December 18, 2014.

protocols and, in some cases, biometric data-sharing agreements with nations being visited by the President. These arrangements would have to take into account the nature of the relationship we have with each country, as well as each nation's legal and privacy environment. Obviously, not all countries will be equally open to our biometrics operations; however, it is safe to say that no country wants to have a U.S. President attacked or killed on its soil, and that would undoubtedly give the United States significant leverage in designing these agreements and protocols. Some nations might be willing to agree to a regular, or even continuous, biometric data exchange, while others might insist on only temporary data sharing in conjunction with a particular presidential visit after which all collected data would be purged.* The scale and scope of these biometric collections would also vary by type of event, location, duration, etc. In some cases, we might defer to the host nation to perform the biometrics collection and matching against any individuals who lack official or diplomatic credentials, with the possible exception of those who will be in direct contact or "dangerously close" to the President.

The following scenario will describe how the USSS could create and execute a program for the use of biometrics to protect the President while abroad. It is broadly based upon the actual events relating to the President's December 2013 South African visit but includes a depiction of how things might have occurred if biometrics had been employed during that event.

## US SECRET SERVICE BIOMETRIC SCENARIO—USSS BIOMETRICS IN ACTION

In 2010, after a number of threats to the President during overseas visits in the mid-late 2000s, the U.S. Secret Service established a comprehensive biometric identification program (known as the "Biometrics for Presidential Security Program" or BPSP) under its Technical Security Division. One of the key technical capabilities of the program was a handheld collection device based upon the Crossmatch SEEK system supported by a briefcase-sized satellite communications system for sending biometric collections

* The United States has a number of similar data-sharing agreements with its closest allies for counterterrorism or law enforcement purposes. The Five Country Conference, involving the United States, United Kingdom, Australia, New Zealand, and Canada, is an example of one such agreement.

from anywhere in the world back to the United States for processing and matching. BPSP representatives worked with their counterparts at the FBI, DoD, DHS, and certain U.S. Intelligence Community members to develop policies and processes to allow USSS biometric collections to be matched against all existing U.S. Government biometric databases and for the resultant match reports to be rapidly returned. A Biometrics Threat Division was also established within the Secret Service's National Threat Assessment Center, which worked with these same U.S. agencies to create a series of country and regionally focused biometrics watchlists. These USSS BEWLs would include the biometrics from identified foreign threat personalities (mostly top tier terrorists or those who had made specific threats to the President) and certain local violent criminals when possible.* These watchlists were uploaded into the Service's SEEK devices prior to each overseas presidential visit and updated as changes occurred.

The most challenging part of the BPSP's mission was the development of biometrics data-sharing agreements with the governments of countries to be visited by the President. In many cases, these were agreements that were designed as adjuncts to existing criminal, military, and intelligence-sharing arrangements, but in some cases they had to be developed from scratch, particularly when the target country had not been visited recently. These agreements provided the framework to determine the type of data that would be shared, when it would be shared (systematically or as needed), and data retention policies. Where possible, data-sharing arrangements were supported by operational protocols that specified the target categories for collection as well as the division of effort between the host nation and the USSS. These protocols were highly flexible given the need to adjust them quickly to the circumstances of a particular event, but they provided a mechanism for the Secret Service's Advance Team to use when planning and preparing for an overseas presidential event.

The BPSP had just become fully operational when the death of former South African President Mandela was announced. Fortunately, this event did not come as a complete surprise, and the Secret Service had already conducted extensive discussions with the South African Government on the role the U.S. President would likely play in the memorial services and related activities following the death of the country's former president and international icon. Those discussions included an agreement on biometric data exchanges and on the biometric collection process that would

* This arrangement was dependent upon the availability of criminal biometrics data from a particular nation hosting a presidential visit.

be included in security operations for President Obama's visit. One part of that agreement was for the South African Department of Home Affairs (DHA) to provide to the United States the biometrics on visitors from select third-party countries who arrived in South Africa within 10 days of an announced visit by the President.* This data transfer was initiated almost immediately upon Nelson Mandela's death and was supported by a BPSP team that deployed to work alongside DHA's biometric technicians to help facilitate the data transfer. This effort resulted in the interdiction of a group of individuals from Nigeria, who had been previously watch-listed due to their suspected association with the Islamic extremist group Boko Haram. These individuals were questioned, refused entry into the country, and returned to Nigeria.

The United States–South Africa biometrics agreement also specified the procedures for collecting biometrics in South Africa to include which kinds of collections would be done by which country. The South Africans agreed to the standard BPSP arrangement that called for the host nation to biometrically screen all nonofficial persons who would have sustained access to the President but who would be outside of the immediate security perimeter (typically considered to be 50 feet). BPSP biometrics technicians would screen individuals within the perimeter who lacked official vetting (e.g., not government officials or accredited foreign diplomats). The two countries also agreed to establish a number of jointly operated long-range facial recognition systems. Just prior to the start of the memorial service, South African security police detained an individual who was initially identified as the sign-language interpreter for the event but whose fingerprints did not match the ones on his national ID card. Subsequent investigation revealed that the individual possessed a stolen and altered ID. It was also discovered that he had been previously charged with murder and was assessed to be mentally unstable.

The President's decision to spend the night in the South African capital required the Secret Service and its South African counterparts to activate another part of the biometric security agreement, which detailed screening procedures for hotel staffs. Like the procedure for the memorial

* DHA operates a biometrics system known as the Home Affairs National Identification System (HANIS). This AFIS-based identification system was designed, integrated, deployed, and supported by a U.S. company, Unisys Corp. The solution captures ten fingerprints per individual, ensures fingerprint quality, extracts fingerprint templates, and performs a 1:N biometric match against the entire database. The system is capable of enrolling up to 60,000 persons daily and over 34 million persons had already been enrolled in HANIS by early 2014.

event, this agreement called for the South Africans to screen all hotel staff members except those who would have direct access to the floor of the hotel where the President would be staying, as well as restaurant staff if he chose to dine in the hotel restaurant. The Secret Service would once again biometrically screen all employees who would have close access to the President including maids, room service personnel, waiters and chefs. The initial screening was actually done the day prior to the President's arrival by BPSP personnel on the USSS Advance Team and South African security personnel. All those employees who were biometrically screened were given biometrically-enabled access badges, which would allow their identities to be quickly verified when arriving at work, before being allowed near the President, or during random spot checks for the duration of the U.S. President's visit. This screening/identity verification process averted what could have been a dangerous situation when one of the room service personnel was checked before being allowed onto President's floor and it was discovered that his iris scan did not match the iris template stored on his access badge even though he looked exactly like the picture on the front of the badge. He was detained and his fingerprints collected, which matched a list of criminals provided to the United States by the South African government. As it turned out, he was a senior member of a local white-supremist Afrikaner organization, who was suspected of involvement in attacks on a number of black South African political figures. Is also turns out that his identical twin was a hotel employee, and he was the one who was initially screened and badged earlier in the week. A search of his car and home revealed numerous weapons and bomb-making materials, and both he and his brother were arrested.

Nothing in the above scenario is beyond the current state of biometrics technology, with the possible exception of the long-range facial recognition technology, which has been the subject of a great deal of research and development and may not be far off. Moreover, the increased use of biometrics for both immigration/border control and for national identification purposes means that biometrics data holdings will continue to grow worldwide—the only complicated issue is gaining access to that data. Despite these complications, the United States has successfully established biometrics data-sharing arrangements with a variety of countries for military and homeland security purposes so there is no reason why similar agreements could not be developed to ensure the safety of the most powerful person in the world. But first, the Secret Service needs to develop a vision and a strategy for biometrically enabled presidential security operations, both of which appear to be absent today.

# 8

# The Future of the U.S. Military Biometrics Capability

The proper use of biometrics can have a profound impact in any military operation from combat missions to humanitarian operations. Military forces in the future will often face a foe and a local populace that they need to understand on a much deeper level than has been the case in past conflicts. Who is a friend? Who is a foe? Who do I already know? Who is hiding their true identity? Answering these questions quickly, accurately, and across great spans of time and distance is what biometrics can do for us. In fact, there have been many instances in which biometric collections performed in Iraq and Afghanistan and shared across multiple USG (U.S. Government) agencies provided the key information that allowed our homeland security elements to deny entry into the United States to individuals who were lying about their backgrounds and personal histories. This information has also been used to deny refugee status to persons who may have intended to do harm here in the United States.

There is a reason that law enforcement agencies around the world have been using fingerprints and, increasingly, other biometric means of identifying criminals for a hundred years—because they work. However, the successful use of biometrics by military forces does not just happen. It requires detailed planning and preparation, not just in terms of the technology but with regards to the supporting policies and the operational procedures. These critical details need to be worked out well in advance of a military mission and captured in military doctrine and unit operating procedures so that a military force can begin using biometrics to its maximum effectiveness immediately upon the start of the mission—not months or years later.

The good news is that developing an effective military biometrics capability is not rocket science. But it does require a bit of forethought, which addresses questions and issues such as

- What missions will benefit from biometrics capabilities (e.g., defensive, offensive, supporting)?
- What kind of data will I collect and use in my identification and verification efforts?
- How much data on the target population do I already have, and who else has data that I can acquire?
- Do I have the right equipment for my missions?
- Do I have the right communications capability and capacity?

Answering these questions will allow a force to structure its biometrics capability properly and to ensure that all operational plans address biometrics data/equipment/communications requirements and specify the types of biometric activities that will take place. And, perhaps most importantly, answering these questions will help provide the basis for the preparation of the force through the development of tactics, techniques and procedures, and the subsequent training in their application. There is no technical substitute for a well-prepared and well-trained force.

Unfortunately, one of the key lessons of the last 10 years of biometric use in combat is that we were largely not a well-prepared and -trained force and thus were not able to take full advantage of these powerful capabilities. It is also unfortunate that this shortcoming is likely to continue in the U.S. DoD (Department of Defense) for the foreseeable future because of an apparent lack of dedication to maintaining a viable operational biometrics capability in the coming postwar period of fiscal constraints and force-structure reductions. At the time of this writing, the Army has essentially shelved its long-standing effort to produce a joint handheld biometrics collection system, known as the Joint Personnel Identification System (JPI). It has also apparently put on hold the acquisition of a follow-on to the current ABIS system—the Biometric Enabling Capability (BEC). I led the development of the operational requirements for both of these systems when I joined the Biometrics Task Force in 2007. Seven years later, the future for both appears to be in question.

As I stated in the Preface, my intent with this book was not for it to be a retrospective on DoD biometrics. Most of us who have been in the military biometrics business for a while have seen more than our share of disfunctionality, struggles over authorities and responsibilities between and within organizations, and the overall lack of a unified vision for the DoD. Despite this, the need for the mission continues and so should the acquisition and development of the necessary technology. Unfortunately, from my perspective and that of others whose knowledge and objectivity I respect, it does not appear that the current DoD acquisition system is up to the task of providing what our forces need now, or what they will need in the future.*

I'm not by any means an acquisition expert; however, I have participated directly in the process, both as a developer and coordinator of operational requirements and as a member of a "customer" in the field, so I think I have some relevant insights. My first insight comes from my direct involvement in the formal requirements documentation process in which I learned first-hand how difficult and time-consuming it is to develop, document, coordinate, and get agreement on operational requirements for a system that the DoD intends to develop and/or acquire. Part of this difficulty stems from the fact that each of the main user communities often have significantly different requirements and meeting them all with a single system would likely result either in the least common denominator approach, in which no one gets everything they need, or an overly expensive system with features that address all possible user requirements, even for those that don't really need them. This difficulty is magnified by the high-tech nature of biometrics technology, the rapid and continuous development of new biometric systems, and the constant application of biometrics technology to supporting new mission sets. Even if the formal requirements development process could produce a set of operational requirements acceptable to all stakeholders (an unlikely occurrence from my perspective), by the time they were formally approved and adopted, they would be outdated and/or insufficient. The military's formal acquisition and development process clearly cannot keep pace with improvements in biometrics technology and the establishment of new missions (Figure 8.1).

* There has been growing criticism of the military acquisition and development process over the past few years, with particular emphasis on the inability of the formal process to keep up with technical developments. In July 2014, a defense industry group, the Professional Services Council, issued its "Acquisition and Technology Policy Agenda." The document states, among other things, that the "increasingly rapid evolution of technology demands an acquisition system that has speed, agility, transparency, competitiveness, and an acceptance for managed levels of risk."

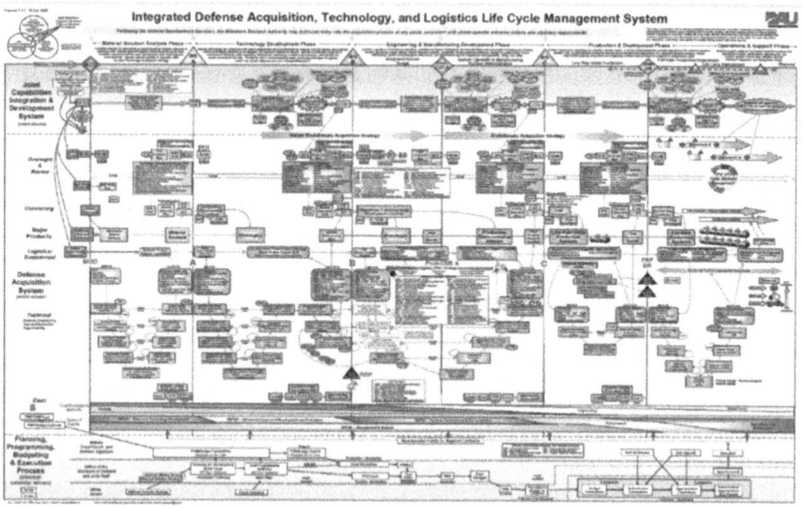


**Figure 8.1** The official DoD acquisition/support process—a process only a battled-hardened DoD bureaucrat could love (or even understand).

## PERSONAL VIGNETTE: "MANAGING" THE REQUIREMENTS PROCESS

During my time as the BTF lead for biometrics requirements ('07-'08), one incident stands out as exemplifying the challenges with this critical element in the DoD acquisition process, and it concerned developing the operational requirements for the previously mentioned Joint Personnel Identification system (JPI). After spending months coordinating this effort across the services, including holding two separate multiday offsite workshops involving all services and agency stakeholders, I was ready to participate in the first formal step of the joint requirements-approval process, where our list of agreed-upon joint requirements would be presented to the Pentagon's Joint Requirements Oversight Council (JROC). The meeting was scheduled for the afternoon, but early in the morning of the meeting day I received a call from the Army staff telling me to come immediately to the Pentagon to deal with a problem with our proposal. When I got there I was told that despite the months of joint efforts and agreed upon requirements development, the Navy had decided to nonconcur with the list of requirements, apparently because they still felt that all their needs were not being addressed and were also concerned that the Army (which was the responsible service for joint biometrics capability development) would take too long to develop a system, while the Navy claimed they had one ready to be built. Not wanting to appear as if the Army screwed this up, my Army staff colleagues and I came up with a proposal by which we would allow the Navy to initially field its own system that would be called JPI-V1 (*aka* Version 1) while the Army would develop the follow-on "joint" system that would be called JPI-V2 and which would incorporate the Navy's unique requirements. The Navy accepted this "compromise" and developed a system for its own use. The Army recently cancelled its JPI-V2 effort.

Another problem with the current acquisition system is that the use of biometrics does not fall cleanly within a single mission area and thus it is difficult to determine which military functional area should pay for it. I observed this situation personally when I went to a meeting at the Pentagon shortly after being assigned to the BTF, during which we discussed a proposed biometrics system fielding plan from the Army. The plan would have put collection systems in most combat units where they should be in order to maximize opportunities for collection. The meeting was being directed by the Army office in charge of planning and funding Army programs (*aka* G-8). The Colonel presiding over the meeting identified himself as being the lead for Army intelligence programs, and that is when I sensed we were in trouble. The reason for my concern was that we were not trying to field a system for intelligence organizations but rather one that would be used more by combat arms units. Unfortunately, the Army at the time classified biometrics collection as an intelligence capability. It soon became clear that asking Army intelligence to pay for systems to be fielded in infantry units was not going to happen, nor was asking the Army combat arms program representatives to pay for what the Army viewed as an "intelligence" system a realistic alternative. That fielding plan did not last long after that meeting and the Army has never come up with another.

The difficulty of placing biometrics within the rigid confines of the Army structure is compounded by the fact that these capabilities are relatively low-volume and low-cost systems, which means low status for anyone who is the owner/sponsor. It's considered career-enhancing to manage a multibillion dollar program that produces thousands of highly-visible and high-cost systems, preferably those that make things go "boom." But no acquisition officer's career is going to be benefitted by managing a program that produces hundreds of relatively cheap, computer "gizmos" that most people, including much of the user base, don't really understand. Moreover, these technologies are not, by and large, produced by the traditional military industrial base but by smaller commercial companies and are bought largely as is (e.g., Commercial Off-the-Shelf/COTS) or with minimal government-performed modification. Developers want to develop so it's hard to get people in the military development business to get excited about a capability that is basically bought and used as is, or with relatively quick and low-cost modifications.

Finally, even when we have asked the formal acquisition/development system to modify an existing biometrics system or to add additional features, it has often proven itself to be not up to the task. In Chapter 3, I described my own personal experience with the "Mobile BAT" (Biometric Automated Toolset) system while working for Task Force Biometrics in Afghanistan. Even after we had discussed the issue with the Army biometrics program office and given them "the plans" for constructing the kits, we could still not get them to produce these for us.* This was by no means the only issue in which the Task Force could not get effective support from the program managers on our technical needs, although most were actually quite minor requirements, such as making alterations to the system coding. We normally just ended up doing them ourselves.

Now, I do not believe that the problems I observed regarding the lack of support from the formal program management structure are reflective of bad intentions or other negative factors on the part of anyone involved. I think that it's just the nature of a system that is not designed to rapidly adapt to changes in operational requirements, the identification of new systems requirements or deficiencies, or the addition of new missions. On the other hand, when biometrics systems are managed by those outside of the formal development structure, rapid and responsive system changes have occurred. One of the primary early developers of the BAT system when it was still an advanced technology demonstration project, Anthony

* This issue had actually been first raised by our forces in Iraq a few years before as an urgent operational requirement. I presided over a number of joint biometrics requirements meetings in which it was discussed, but for reasons I do not fully understand to this day, it was never submitted and accepted as a formal requirement or acted upon.

Iasso, described making changes to the system while on the phone with users and even creating entirely new mission capabilities virtually overnight. I know just enough about things like "configuration management" and "network certification" to know that such a "Wild West" approach to system development can be dangerous. However, I also know that once the BAT was put under the formal acquisition and program management system, development essentially ceased, and there was much less responsiveness to user concerns (Figure 8.2).

I have noted that there are ways to perform rapid system developments and modifications outside of the formal acquisition and development process. There are also ways to make rapid purchases and fielding of existing commercially developed systems outside of the traditional acquisition process using an organization like the Army's Rapid Equipping Force (REF). The REF was created in 2002, initially to rapidly respond to the urgent needs of forces fighting in Afghanistan, but it quickly grew to become a major fielder of CIED (Counter Improvised Explosive Device) technologies in Iraq and provider of advanced personal equipment for Army personnel in Iraq and Afghanistan. The REF also helped to get some biometrics systems into the field. The REF operates outside of the Army's traditional program structure, and many thought it would go away once the wars in Iraq and Afghanistan were over; however, the Army REF website states that it will continue to operate in the postwar period.

## DoD BIOMETRICS NEEDS AN AGILE ACQUISITION PROGRAM

So what are we to do with a set of capabilities that, like the misfit toys of Rudolph the Red-Nosed Reindeer, "just don't fit?" We need some way of assessing our biometrics needs, identifying and rapidly purchasing available systems, making or directing modifications, and funding the development of advanced technologies and applications. Shortly before I sat down to write this section, I had a conversation with a good friend, biometrics guru, and former BTF colleague, Benji Hutchinson, and he said that he had been having similar thoughts and had started talking about "Agile Development." So, I decided to appropriate that phrase and modify it to describe an *Agile Acquisition Program (AAP)* for defense biometrics. Such a program would incorporate some of the aspects of traditional program management, which emphasizes the long-term development and management of a capability along with stable and sustained funding, but it would

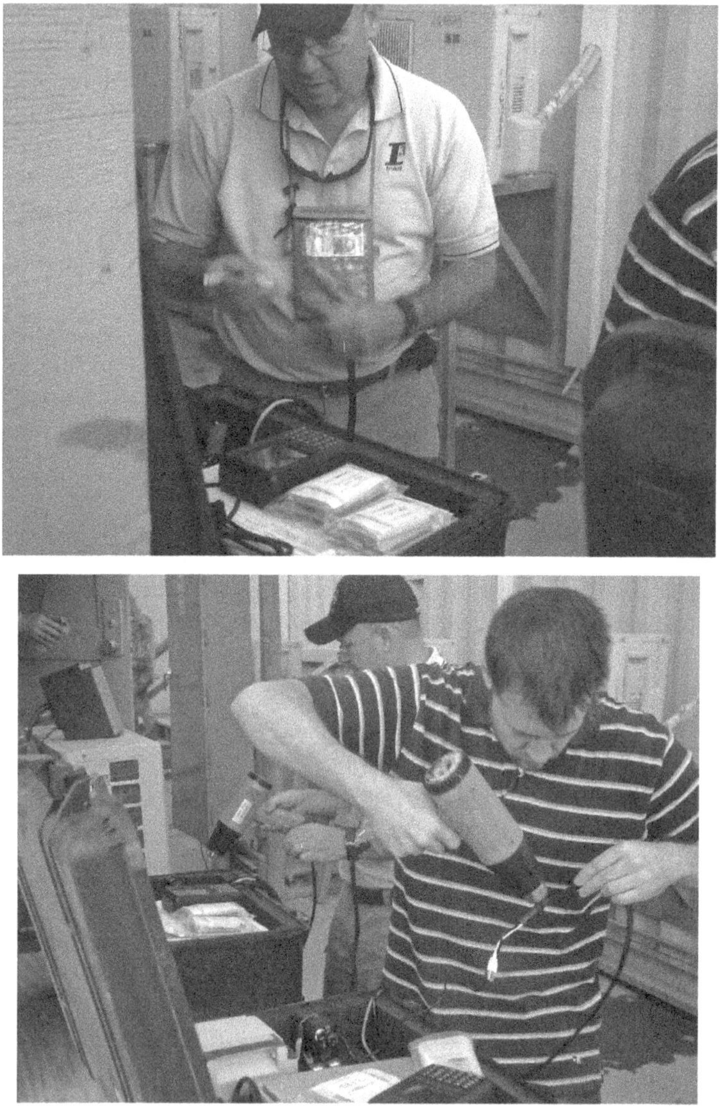

**Figure 8.2** Members of Task Force Biometrics contrasting mobile BAT kits. The Army's formal acquisition process often could not deliver the biometrics capabilities required by the field in a timely manner.

add an REF-like ability to support rapid requirements development, acquisition, and fielding. The new Army Biometrics AAP would do the following:

- *Establish a minimum set of mandatory operational standards* (mostly software and data related) and testing standards for approved systems. These standards would only be those that are critical to ensure data quality, uniformity, and completeness, which would maximize the ability to share DoD biometrics data with other systems across the DoD and with key U.S. and allied partners. The list of standards would not include "form" or "fit" issues, such as size and weight, water resistance, color, modalities collected, etc. Those would be left to the user organizations.
- *Manage an approved products list.* If a system is not on the list, it cannot be acquired. Each system would have to meet the mandatory requirements described above in order to be "certified" and added to the list. But again, those requirements would be minimal.
- *Manage evolving operational requirements.* This would not be the kind of formal requirements development and validation process in which I participated because in the end each potential user organization would need to develop its own specific requirements for things like form, fit, and function. However, this process would help provide guidance for commercial developers to use as they develop new systems or modify existing ones. Essentially, the program manager office would be the interface between the user community and industry, and would provide guidance to each.
- *Provide funding for limited product operational testing and pilot projects.* Systems will need to be operationally tested before they can be put on the approved products list, and there may need to be pilot deployments for those systems that may see large-scale acquisition. The program manager (PM) office can provide expertise and objective, unbiased testing to supplement a service or an agency's testing capability.
- *Assist users in rapidly acquiring capabilities for operational needs.* Users would provide the funding for system purchase and the "Bio AAP" would provide the mechanism for rapid purchasing and fielding.

Unlike a traditional PM system, this AAP would provide more of an acquisition framework within which a potential user (and system vendor) would need to operate, rather than being involved in the development process directly. Beyond that, it would leave decisions and funding in the hands of the user, which could be a Service-level entity, a Combatant Command (COCOM), or a joint force deployed on an operational mission. The key element I want to highlight is that the AAP is really only managing the standards, and to a lesser extent the requirements, from a long-term perspective along with providing funding to sustain some research and operational evaluations. They would also provide advice and assistance to the actual users as well as some guidance to the commercial sector. If this makes sense for biometrics, and I'll leave that up to the reader to decide, it may be a model for similar high tech, "misfit toys" that are now in use across the DoD.

A new program structure with long-term funding will not only ensure that the right biometric systems are available at the right time, but it will also help ensure that biometrics are institutionalized within the Services. Institutionalization will lead to the development of operational policies and procedures and the execution of formal training programs. If this occurs, then the future of DoD biometrics will be a bright one, and we'll have the right systems, at the right time, in the hands of units capable of using them to their maximum effectiveness.

I wish I could just leave on the positive vision I articulated above, but my experience has unfortunately left me with a less sanguine outlook. In fact, I'd have to say that the possibility that DoD will retain anything like a Department-wide biometrics capability is about 50–50. I think it's just as likely that the Army will give up on its effort to maintain a separate DoD biometrics database and will look for a way to transfer the data to another USG element, potentially the DoJ (Department of Justice) or DHS (Department of Homeland Security). From a purely technical and strategic standpoint, that might not be such a bad thing, particularly if the DoD maintains the ability to ensure that military missions are adequately supported.* My biggest concern with this scenario is that the Services (particularly the Army) will not develop the kinds of operational processes, policies and training programs that build on what we have learned over the past decade of war, which means that we'll have to learn how to fight with biometrics all over again the next time we conduct a major military operation. Hopefully, there will be pockets of capability that continue within the special forces and intelligence mission areas that can be leveraged and built upon when we go to war the next time (as we always do).

* One way to do this would be to embed a customer-facing element within the data-hosting organization to help ensure that military users' needs are supported. This element could also manage some of the DoD-unique services, such as the BEWL (Biometrics-Enabled Watchlist), and provide certain kinds of forensic support.

When that time comes, I hope that some of the lessons I have articulated here and that have been captured elsewhere can help ensure an integrated and well-prepared approach to biometrics to protect our forces and defeat our enemies.

## PERSONNEL SUPPORT FOR FUTURE BIOMETRICS OPERATIONS

As I've discussed previously, the U.S. military began operations in Afghanistan and Iraq with no significant biometrics capability. The rapid but steady process of acquiring technology and the personnel to operate much of it fell greatly upon the ranks of a contractor-led force. The lead biometric organizations for both combat theaters were almost totally comprised of contracted personnel with a small group of military or government-civilian personnel in key leadership positions, and this did not change throughout the course of Operation Iraqi Freedom or Operation Enduring Freedom in Afghanistan.*

Given the newness of biometrics to the U.S. military, and the rapid technical and operational development that occurred once it began to be used in combat, it is understandable that an army of contractors would have been initially used to provide critical biometric support functions; however, I fault the DoD for not developing an internal biometric workforce over time. While I do not want to disparage the (for the most part) excellent work done by dedicated men and women in the biometric contractor community, I have to call attention to some of the downsides to this over-reliance upon nonmilitary personnel in providing direct support to combat operations. To begin with, contract personnel cost the U.S. taxpayer double or triple what similar level military or government civilian personnel would have cost. That this cost was relatively slight, compared to the overall hundreds of billions spent on other costs associated with our decade of combat operations, does not make it less noteworthy.

Next is the lack of operational flexibility that comes with an overreliance upon contractors. Soldiers are used to frequent changes of mission

* When I was in Afghanistan in 2009, we had about 10 military or government personnel in Task Force Biometrics and over 200 contract employees. Contractors provided all of the services directly in support of Coalition military units including operating biometric base access systems at the larger facilities (not part of the TF), training military system operators, and performing field technical support functions.

and even of basic tasks, such as the armor and artillery units that were ordered to park their heavy equipment in Iraq and to conduct what were essentially infantry operations. Military units and their members will do what they are told, even if it is not what they were really trained to do; but the same cannot be said of contractors. Contractors perform functions listed in a contract's Statement of Work, which is not something that can normally be changed quickly (if at all) or without (oftentimes) significant costs. Additionally, and perhaps more importantly, aside from those contractors working for security companies like the infamous Blackwater, most contract employees are not permitted to carry weapons even when operating in combat zones. This was to have a negative impact upon the Task Force Biometrics' ability to fully carry out the previously discussed Theater Biometrics Campaign Plan. The ability to execute some of the more ambitious collection missions, such as those in the larger Afghan prisons, were forestalled by the inability to provide security protection for the unarmed contractors who were to do the enrollments. In fact, the overwhelming contractor make-up of TF Bio was to be an issue of great concern to Admiral Harward when he took command of the TF's higher headquarters. He recognized almost immediately that having to use contractors to execute the kinds of biometrics missions he wanted to execute was going to be a serious constraint on the overall effectiveness of biometric operations across the country.*

The final problem with depending upon contractors as a long-term manpower solution is that the military does not have the benefit of building the full range of biometric skills that will be required if biometrics is to remain a military capability that will be retained after combat operations are over. I also believe that having contractors in direct support of combat units has a negative impact on the integration of biometrics into the full range of military missions that I have described in the book. Having someone else do your biometrics for you, does not give you "skin in the game," and I believe this is in part the reason the Army has had a tough time making biometrics an enduring capability.

Now, despite the negative consequences of an over-reliance on contractors for biometrics operations, it does not appear that any of the services are going to create a corps of specially trained biometrics personnel,

* The bulk of the Task Force's personnel outside of the main headquarters at Bagram Airbase and the secondary office on Kandahar Airfield consisted of contractor Field Support Representatives (FSR) whose job was to support military units with system operator training, minor equipment repair, and database maintenance. While they were not supposed to perform biometrics collections themselves, this did occasionally occur.

so it is likely that any future large-scale combat operation will have to call upon contractor support, at least initially. However, this does not have to be the kind of open-ended situation that we saw in Iraq and Afghanistan. I believe a sensible alternative would be to start with a contractor force to do the technical field support and some kinds of enrollment activities (large base access, for example), while at the same time having the same contract companies train military personnel to assume many/most of the direct combat unit support after a set period of time. The military personnel that would be trained and eventually deployed for biometrics support could be from the reserve forces or from military units that are unlikely to be deployed, such as certain shore-based Navy support units or U.S.-based Air Force elements. From what I have seen, even those fairly technical tasks performed by biometrics FSRs (Field Support Representatives) are tasks that we could teach any fairly intelligent soldier, sailor, airman, or marine in a relatively short amount of time, and having these missions performed by military personnel would overcome the negative consequences of using contractors that I discussed above.*

* Many of the biometrics support contractors I met were not from technical backgrounds but were former military personnel from a variety of specialties, including many from the combat arms fields. In Afghanistan, one of the leads for the main Task Force Biometrics contract had been an Army truck driver. Biometrics may be somewhat technical in nature but it's not rocket science or brain surgery.

# 9

# Afterword
## The U.S. Department of Defense Needs an Advanced Identity Enterprise

Military biometrics is a fast moving, ever-evolving capability area. In this book I've articulated what in most cases are accepted and, to some extent actually practiced, operational employments. Unfortunately, technology developments tend to move much faster than the development of operational concepts, no matter how well formulated. So, before I close the main portion of my book, I want to discuss my evolving thoughts on what I believe should be the long-term, strategic goal of our military identity efforts—the establishment of an Advanced Identity Enterprise or AIE.

We need an AIE first and foremost because the operational environment is changing and this will have significant impacts on how we collect biometric and other identity data in the future and how we make use of this data. We also need the ability to make use of biometric data that we do not collect or store ourselves, but that are present in databases we can access if we have an enterprise designed to do so. The technology of identification is also changing so rapidly and continually that we need the ability to quickly integrate new collection platforms and new kinds of data, which we have either not collected before or are not actively used as part of our automated identification process. And finally, and perhaps most importantly, we need an enterprise that integrates the operational aspects of identification with the intelligence and analytical process, so that we have a seamless ops–intel approach to military identification that operates across all classification levels.

The AIE I am proposing would be based upon the following five key elements:

1. An open and flexible architecture that will allow external elements to plug in, play and unplug, based upon a "Bring Your Own Device," "Bring Your Own Data," and "Bring Your Own Business" rules framework
2. Full integration of operational and intelligence capabilities, functions, and processes
3. An expanded concept of "enrollment"
4. An advanced approach to identification that incorporates the use of nonbiometric identity data and, when possible, the fusion of nonbiometric and biometric matching
5. *True identification* that moves beyond "One-to-Many" towards "One-to-All"

## OPEN AND FLEXIBLE ARCHITECTURE

I mentioned right up front in this book that I am not by nature, education, or training a technical person. As a result, this chapter and this section, in particular, was very challenging for me to write. Still, I did serve briefly at the BTF as the acting Division Chief in charge of Architecture and Standards and have picked up a thing or two since then, so if I stick more to *what* the system should do and not *how*, I think I'll be okay.

Wikipedia defines a system architecture as: "the conceptual model that defines the structure, behavior, and more views of a system." I think of the architecture of a complex information technology system such as biometrics as the nervous system that ties (hopefully) all of the elements together so that they can exchange data effectively and efficiently. An architecture is made up of physical infrastructure, data formatting standards, processes and business rules that allow all of the pieces to interact towards some central goal or purpose. From what I have seen, our biometrics architectures, not only in the DoD but elsewhere in the USG, have been inwardly focused and insular and not designed to facilitate incorporating data, processes, and systems from "outsiders," complicating the ability to work with both US and foreign allies alike and to rapidly incorporate new capabilities. I have already discussed some of the challenges we have experienced in DoD biometrics in that regard.

There is a lot of talk in the IT world lately about the trend towards open architecture systems, which Wikipedia defines as "a type of computer architecture or software architecture that is designed to make adding, upgrading and swapping components easy." On a conceptual level, such a system is what we need in the DoD, not just because is it trendy, but for significant operational reasons. The principal reason to build such a system is the need to be able to incorporate data from as many systems and sources as possible in order to be able to have the widest possible set of identity data to support the various military operations I've discussed in this book. However, it is not enough to simply be able to take in data; the system also must be built to accommodate the unique policies and restrictions that may come with using some kinds of data, particularly that which may be provided by foreign partner militaries or nonmilitary elements. It is important, therefore, that our system be flexible enough to incorporate new business rules regarding with whom data can be shared, how it will be shared, and how long it will be retained in the system. What I am articulating is something built around the broad capabilities of the ISAF (International Security Assistance Forces) ABIS system I described back in Chapter 3, and will also cover in more detail in Appendix E.

Since coalition operations are the way we fight in large- and even small-scale military operations, our biometrics enterprise architecture needs to be built to support them. The architecture should allow allied countries to use whatever systems they bring to the fight, and provide a mechanism to format and normalize the data, so that it can be shared across the enterprise. Each nation should also be able to bring, or build, its own data repository that could be rapidly integrated into the U.S. architecture. And finally, each nation should be able to control access to and usage of their data based upon their own business rules, many of which could probably be built in advance as part of the architecture and modified and "turned on" when needed. This "bring your own" approach will reduce the need to build mission-unique biometrics databases and shorten the time for a future coalition operation to become fully supported by biometrics.

## INTEGRATED BIOMETRICS OPERATIONS AND INTELLIGENCE

I first mentioned the critical relationship between biometrics operations and the associated intelligence analysis in Chapter 2, but I also noted that significant conflict existed between the two sides of the military identification coin. As one of the few people in DoD with significant experience in both the biometrics operational and intelligence worlds, I have come to understand that when it comes to the use of biometrics for military operations, *biometrics needs intelligence to be meaningful and intelligence needs biometrics to be actionable.* In other words, I can have all kinds of biometric data on John Smith, but if I have nothing tying him to any particular activity or event, all I can really use it for is to confirm every time I encounter him that he is till John Smith. This may be useful for some missions but will not be particularly helpful if John is a bad guy. On the other hand, I may have an incredible dossier on Mr. Smith that lists in exhaustive detail all of his nefarious activities, but unless I can link this information to his biometrics, it will probably not help me if Mr. Smith is subsequently encountered by a soldier in the field, by a guard at a gate access point, or by an immigration officer at JFK Airport.

So clearly, in order for our military identification system to be operationally useful, we need both biometrics and intelligence. Unfortunately, our current biometric "enterprise" is not built that way. Instead, we have created biometrics and intelligence processes and capabilities as if they should operate separately, which in fact they largely do. The result is a Rube Goldberg-like structure that delays or even denies the reporting of critical information to people who need it in a timely fashion, and which requires numerous manpower-intensive manual processes to get the results we do. My solution is for the next generation of the DoD biometrics repository to be designed with an analytical capability embedded into the architecture. This capability would do the following:

1. Provide a case file for all new enrollments, based upon a single common identification number like the global unique ID (GUID) associated with each enrollment
2. Serve as the internal case management tool for all analysis of the biometrics files
3. Allow, via a web interface, external customers to have immediate visibility on any new enrollment being ingested into the system (e.g., intelligence analysts, military units, other USG Agencies)
4. Depict all contextual, biological, and biographical data associated with the enrollment in a series of searchable and relatable fields
5. Provide the *common identity platform* with instantiations across all classification domains. This would allow
   a. A single reference point (*aka* Common Identity Picture) for each unique identity in our database

b. Appropriate analysts at any level to append relevant information and analysis to each "case"
c. Data entered at any level to replicate up to the domains at higher classification levels
d. Allow identities to be centrally managed and assigned to individuals or organizations based upon relevant policies and guidance
e. Enable each identity to be linked to those existing in other intelligence databases

This system would allow a unit intelligence officer to immediately see that an enrollment occurred of an individual in his area of operations who was suspected of involvement in IED manufacture even if no match occurred. He could also request to be notified of any change to the case made in the future, such as a match to a latent print. It would also allow an agency like the DIA to assign identities for analysis and production by location and identity type (e.g., "military," "terrorist," "scientific and technical," "political," "criminal," etc.) to organizations across the DoD Intelligence Community, just as they now do with the production of formal intelligence products. For example, they could assign all identities associated with regional militaries in South America to the U.S. Southern Command J2 (intelligence staff) that would, in turn, assign them to specific all-source military-capabilities analysts in their organization. This arrangement would provide a structure to the DoD IC's identity analysis effort and, perhaps more importantly, help foster the incorporation of identity intelligence into all standard analytic processes and products. Thus, every all-source intelligence analyst would become in effect an "identity analyst."

## EXPANDING THE CONCEPT OF ENROLLMENT

The next step towards developing our AIE is to dramatically expand our enrollment capability. Typically, enrollment into a biometric database occurs as the result of direct interaction between a biometric system and a subject. This can be an automated (e.g., via a kiosk) or a manual process, but within the military application it has been mostly the latter. The exception to this has been when bulk files of biometric data have been acquired and ingested into a system like ABIS or when paper fingerprint cards have been received, digitized, and "enrolled." For the near- to medium-term, it is unlikely that the United States or its closest allies will be involved in large-scale, lengthy land-force deployments. As a result of the changing operational environment, the opportunities for the direct enrollment of large numbers of individuals will significantly decrease. Ingesting bulk files acquired as the result of data-sharing agreements or via other means (i.e., the "Beg, Buy, or Steal" method) can provide some of our data needs, but what other opportunities are there?

I believe that expanding the concept of "enrollment" is key to ensuring that we are able to continue to populate our military biometrics database after our large-scale overseas military operations are over. In the future, enrollment needs to become a much more flexible process, which is less focused on the kinds of direct biometrics encounters we have had over the past decade, and more focused on making use of identity data that we may already have in our possession, or that may be available to us. Fortunately, there is an abundance of useful personal data on individuals of interest in datasets throughout the DoD and USG, as well as others, that we can potentially access. Many of these datasets actually include a biometric of matchable quality, normally facial photos, but also fingerprints in some cases; but since they are not structured as biometrics databases, this data cannot be directly accessed and used for matching purposes. Instead, we need a process to pull the data from them and to use it to build enrollments.

Another potential category of enrollments are those based upon intelligence analysis and reporting. U.S. intelligence agencies produce thousands of personnel profiles, biographies, and assessments on foreign military members, political figures, criminals, intelligence personnel, and others, and many also include a biometric (photo). It should be possible (and actually quite simple) to allow the analysts producing such person-specific intelligence products to create an enrollment and to submit it to the U.S. ABIS.* Not only will such a process help ensure a constant flow of new identities into our database(s), it will also help to further integrate identity analysis across the intelligence spectrum.

* This process would be web-based and allow the input of available biographical, contextual, and analytical information to an online enrollment form. Any biometrics that would be included, principally facial photos, would need to meet certain guidelines for quality, size and, perhaps, other factors as well.

## BEYOND BIOMETRICS

When I started this project, my working title was the "Military Identity Operations Guide" because, even though this book is almost completely about biometrics, I felt that I needed to address the possible use of nonbiometric identity data in the identification process. I've thought for some time that it might be possible to use some of the nonbiometric data we collect during a typical direct enrollment to support our matching processes. For instance, we could use the biographic, biologic, or contextual data collected during an enrollment to support our latent print matching process or when comparing poorer quality fingerprints or facial photos. At the very least, doing so might assist us with conducting manual comparisons by reducing the number of candidate pairs we need to manually evaluate. Perhaps it might even be possible to collect enough nonbiometric identity information on an individual to achieve a positive identification without even using biometrics?

In the early spring of 2014, shortly after I started working at Unisys Corporation, someone forwarded me a copy of a Request for Information issued previously by the FBI (Federal Bureau of Investigation), which stated that they were studying the possibility of using both biometric and nonbiometric data as part of a future identification capability. I thought this was unusually forward-thinking for the FBI and seemed to be along the lines of what I had been pondering for some time. In a conversation with one of the Unisys identity experts, I learned about a Dutch company called WCC, which had developed a system that employed a multialgorithmic approach to performing multimodel biometrics fusion. The same process could also be used to match other kinds of identity data as well. In fact, as the company representatives explained to me, *any* kind of data that can be associated with an individual can be matched, and the results of that match (i.e., the score) can be fused with the results of the match of any other kind of data including biometrics matches.

Using a system such as this could have a huge impact on military identification. For example, say that I have two images that may be of the same person. One is a high-quality picture from a direct enrollment for base access, which includes all the standard biographical and contextual information. The other is a medium-range and lower-quality photo of an individual suspected of conducting apparent surveillance of a friendly facility overseas. The facial images alone may not of sufficient quality to generate a match from either an automated system or by manual comparison. However, it could be possible to achieve a match using certain biological features evident in the two pictures* and perhaps data regarding the location or other contextual information, and then to fuse the score of that match with the score of the facial image match. The resultant combined match would allow a positive identification to be made. A similar process might also be applied to the latent print-matching process, in order to winnow down the number of candidate pairs requiring manual comparison to just a few, which would allow for a more timely operational decision than is often the case today, using biometric data alone.

## BEYOND ONE-TO-MANY IDENTIFICATION

In Chapter 2, I added a word of caution to the discussion of the concept of "identification" using biometrics, noting that our identification efforts are really only as good as the data in the databases to which we have access. When I'm teaching courses on biometrics, I often highlight the fact that One-to-Many identification is not the same as One-to-Everything (or One-to-All), and that our ability to truly identify an unknown individual is only as good (and complete) as the data to which we have access.† The more I talk about the shortcomings in our biometrics identification scheme, the more I ask myself: Why does it have to be that way? Why can't we go beyond our limited, available datasets towards a much more expansive approach to identification in a combat environment? Can't we get closer to "One-to-All" than we do today? Well, given what I described in the previous section, I believe we can and should.

Incorporating the greater use of nonbiometric data in the identification process will allow a military force to have a much better sense of who the individuals they encounter really are, not just who they say they are when we first encounter them. As I mentioned in Chapter 2, just establishing a single/consistent identity for an individual may be good enough for many identity applications, but certainly not for all of them. For instance, if I'm hiring an individual to perform relatively low-risk work on an overseas base, just knowing that the individual does not have derogatory information in any of my available databases may be good enough. On the other hand, if I'm going to allow him access to sensitive or valuable facilities

* These physical features are sometimes referred to as "soft biometrics" and include traits such as hair color, sex, ethnicity, age, height, etc.

† In Chapter 2, I discussed the issue of One-to-Many "identification" and noted that our current processes only allow us to search against the limited set of data we have in our own databases or a few others to which we may have access.

or information, or provide him with weapons, I may want to know a bit more. Is he lying about his place of birth, current address, school, associates, or other background information? If so, I may not want to hire him or allow him to carry a weapon. Information such as this could be readily gleaned from unclassified or even classified sources, but it is not part of our current automated identification process for those individuals who are not the target of some kind of intelligence effort.* Building such a process into our automated identification efforts would not require a huge amount of resources but it would require recognition that using biometrics alone is not sufficient in all cases. "One-to-Many" is not "One-to-All," and sometimes you need "One-to-All."

The new identification system I've described here will require some new resources in order to provide the more advanced analytical and matching capabilities. But more significantly, it will require a change in the thought patterns that have driven the U.S. DoD approach to tactical identity operations. It will require an acknowledgment that the intelligence aspects of identity operations cannot be developed or executed separately from the collection and matching of the identity data itself. It will require an acceptance of a multiple-domain identification system that can provide a common identity picture across all domains, to facilitate both intelligence analysis and operational usage. It will require a much wider and more flexible approach to enrollment, which will allow us to continue to populate our identity databases without direct access to our enrollees. And, it will require the recognition that biometrics alone are not sufficient for all identification needs, and that we can maximize the matching and the identification processes by making use of a wider set of nonbiometrics data. I believe the technology is ready, but unfortunately, based upon what I have seen in recent presentations from senior DoD biometrics officials, the Department is not.†

* Searching for information on an individual, beyond that provided in a biometrics enrollment, is not part of the operational identification process today but is, instead, performed by intelligence personnel on particular persons of interest and normally performed using classified sources. However, there is no reason why we could not build such a process into our identification system by using open sources, such as social media, to verify the basic identity information provided by an individual during certain kinds of identification activities.

† I've attended presentations by DoD biometrics programs officials describing the follow on system to replace the ABIS and the main theme could be summarized as: "We're going to keep doing what we have been doing but we're going to do it better." I do not believe this is a viable strategy for anything other than a future of irrelevance.

# APPENDIX A: KEY CONCEPTS

The following are the book's key concepts for military identity operations from Chapter 2 through Chapter 7:

Chapter 2 Key Concepts:

- There are important differences between identification and verification and all "identifications" are not the same.
- There are many different ways to collect biometrics and all can be used to support a military operation.
- Modalities matter: Use the right ones for the mission and the environment.
- A "match" is not a sure thing, but it can be very close.
- Forensics is a means of biometrics collection (*aka* "latent biometrics").
- There is a symbiotic relationship between Biometrics and Intelligence.
- Data sharing is critical: across organizations, nations and applications.
- Good communications are critical for effective biometrics operations.
- Biometrics has many uses: offense, defense (i.e., force protection), intelligence, and supporting activities (e.g., medical, resource control/management, border control).

Chapter 3 Key Concepts:

- Biometrics operations must be well planned and prepared for in advance, to include
  - Data type and quantity—
    - Identify biometrics data requirements.
    - Develop a Biometrics Collection Plan.
    - Begin building the database *before* the operation.
  - Collection systems—
    - Choose the right system for the mission or maximize the effectiveness of the systems you have.
  - Matching schemes: on system, with Biometric Enabled Watchlist (BEWL), remote database

- Databases: forward, remote, multinational
- Communications and data movement
- Effective policies
- TTPs and training
- Collection considerations
  - Maximize collection opportunities.
  - Collect the highest quality and most complete set of biometrics possible.

- Modalities matter: The modality must match the mission
- Plan for multinational operations

Chapter 4 Key Concepts:

- Biometrics can play a vital role in the targeting process by adding certainty to the identification of targets and adding speed to the verification of targets.
- The Special Operations Forces need for certainty and speed has made them leaders in the employment of biometrics technologies on the battlefield.
- Biometrics and related intelligence information are critical to the ability to analyze Improvised Explosive Device (IED) networks, identify the critical members and tie them to IED-related incidents.
- Biometrics-enabled checkpoint operations and biometric reconnaissance can support current and future offensive operations, constrain the movement of enemy elements and provide critical intelligence on a local populace.
- Biometrics can have a significant impact on Population Management, which is a key tenet of COIN (counterinsurgency) operations.

Chapter 5 Key Concepts:

- The integration of biometrics into access control systems is vital to the effective protection of friendly personnel, resources and facilities.
- Vetting of local nationals for hiring, contracting for services or training must include the collection and use of biometric data.
- Biometrics can aid in insider threat detection.
- Biometric-enabled checkpoints, or the use of biometrics by screening forces, provides more robust force protection for friendly forces during combat operations.

Chapter 6 Key Concepts:

- Identification and identity verification via biometrics supports detention decision making and the entire detainee management process.
- Border control supported by biometrics can have a significant impact on the movement of enemy personnel and material.
- Biometric support to the legal process became a powerful tool in countering the Iraqi insurgency and has been adopted by the Marines as a key component of their identity operations.
- Biometrics can support humanitarian operations by providing security and controlling access to resources.
- Biometrics could be a powerful tool to verify the identity of friendly forces, track their movements throughout the theater of operations, and enable rapid access to medical data.

Chapter 7 Key Concepts:

- Biometrics will become increasingly important for friendly ("Blue") force applications including personnel management, security, and access control.
- Technologies for stand-off and mobile collection, particularly based upon facial recognition, will improve and become operationally useful.
- There will be improved forensics applications of biometrics, especially rapid DNA processing and matching and automated latent print matching.
- The future will see "biometrics ubiquity" including biometrics embedded in targeting sensors and in sensors for the terminal guidance of munitions.
- Other USG elements have similar needs for identification and identity verification as the military does and should develop their own biometrics capabilities:
  - US State Department: Diplomatic security and support for non-traditional diplomacy
  - US Secret Service: Threat identification and overseas presidential security

# APPENDIX B: COMMON BIOMETRICS MODALITIES EXPLANATION AND THEIR COMPARISON

As I stated in Chapter 2, the number of ways to measure the human body and to use those measurements to identify a person is almost endless. In addition to well-known modalities like fingerprints and face, a great deal of research has gone into studying different and sometimes strange sounding modalities, such as ear lobe, body odor, and heat signature. In this section, I'm going to expand on my earlier comments and will mainly focus on the more mainstream modalities that are actually in use to some extent or are being studied by military organizations.

*Fingerprint:* Fingerprint identification is the Granddaddy of biometrics modalities and is widely, if not universally, employed by law enforcement organizations around the world.* The near-ubiquity of use means that there are lots of data in lots of databases against which newly collected prints can potentially be matched (see Table B.1 for examples of some of the larger fingerprint databases). Fingerprints are also important because of their inherent forensic applications. The technology for automated fingerprint collection and matching is very mature, and despite some recent U.S. criminal cases questioning their accuracy/uniqueness, fingerprints are generally accepted as highly accurate in determining and verifying identity.

One of the drawbacks of fingerprints is their close association with criminal activity, which may cause acceptance problems when attempting to use them as a verification tool only—for access control with a nonthreat population for example. Fingerprints are also susceptible to obscuration due to environmental factors, which may negatively affect their use with

* The Wikipedia page on fingerprints states that they were used as signatures on contracts by Babylonians in the second millennium BCE, which, I guess, would make fingerprints the ancient ancestor of biometric modalities.

**Table B.1** Representative Sample of Fingerprint Files in National Databases

| Country | Name | Number of Fingerprint Records (Est/Approx) | Remarks |
|---|---|---|---|
| International | Interpol | 198,000 (Dec 2013) | Member-countries can submit digital or hard-copy prints for comparison |
| U.S.A. | FBI IAFIS | 78 million (Aug 2014) + 833, 000 unmatched latent prints | Includes criminal and civil ten-print and latent files |
| USA | DHS IDENT | 173 million | Many are two-print files[a] |
| India | Aadhar | 850 million | Supports India's national ID program |
| UK | IDENT1 | 6.5 million | Ten-prints. Also maintains database of palm prints |
| South Africa | HANIS | 30+ million | Planned size of database is up to 50 million |

*Note:* These figures are approximate, from various sources and for broad comparison purposes only.

[a] The IDENT program began in 1997 with 2-print collection. DHS began the transition to 10-print collections in late 2007.

a populace that has a high proportion of manual laborers. They are also more difficult to collect properly without a fair amount of training and experience, particularly when operating in an unsecure environment and dealing with an uncooperative subject. A full fingerprint enrollment will also require more storage space than an enrollment using a number of other modalities such as the iris.* This could be a limiting factor if collecting biometrics using a handheld collection device, which may have limited storage capacity. It is also an issue for large-scale databases that may contain millions of enrollments. It is generally thought that fingerprints do not perform as well in terms of speed and accuracy in larger databases.

*Face:* Facial Recognition (FR) is an area of great interest, in part due to the ease with which facial images can be collected, and the inherent

* Although the size of the individual templates for a single iris and a single fingerprint are roughly similar, you only need two for a full iris enrollment while you'll need ten for a full ten-print enrollment.

ability to collect images from a distance and even covertly. Collecting match-quality facial photos can be done with a wide variety of camera types, including a web camera attached to a PC (personal computer) or various video recording devices. However, as a rule of thumb, higher quality images will produce better results in an automated facial recognition system, so it is always best to use the highest quality camera possible. Moreover, because a good camera can be fit with an even better long-range lens, there is an inherent capability to collect matchable facial images from a distance, which provides for both the security of standoff separation of collector and target, and the potential ability to collect the image covertly.* That being said, the best results are obtained from images collected in a controlled environment which can ensure that all measurable features are evident, sufficiently illuminated, and clearly captured.† These requirements place some limits on the viability of FR for many military applications at present.‡ Developments in improved optics and advanced image processing techniques that support matching of off-angle facial images (i.e., not straight-on full-face or full-profile images like typical "mug shots"), such as the use of 3D modeling, will gradually increase the operational utility of facial recognition for many military applications. Despite the current technical limitations on automated matching, faces are an important thing to capture because of their inherent usefulness as a low-tech visual identification/verification tool, and also because combining even a poor quality image with other biometrics or even nonbiometrics data (which I will discuss below) may increase the matching accuracy when using a system that employs biometric fusion.

---

* Collecting facial images is also generally not considered particularly invasive since there is no contact needed between the sensor and the subject, although it can be a problem in cultures where many women are veiled.

† Automated facial recognition systems operate best with front-facing images taken at the same level as the camera. These provide the best way to accurately perform the feature measurements most systems rely on, such as the distance between the eyes, distance between the corners of the mouth, etc.

‡ There are also few national or international standards for facial recognition, which makes the evaluation of automated and manual FR somewhat challenging. INTERPOL, the international law enforcement agency, recently announced it had held a meeting that "gathered 24 technical and biometrics experts and examiners from 16 countries who produced a 'best practice guide' for the quality, format and transmission of images to be used in facial recognition." Unlike the case with fingerprint examiners, there are no formally recognized certification programs for manual facial recognition.

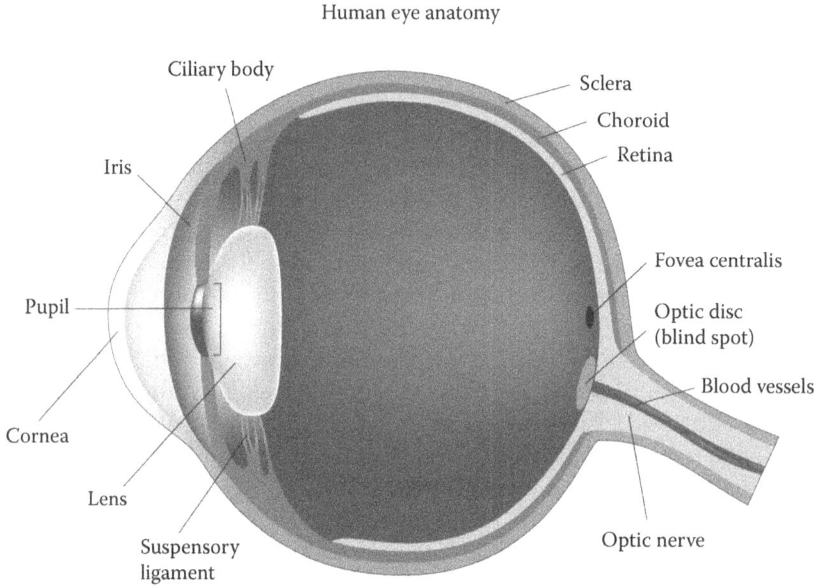


**Figure B.1** Key structures of the eye.

*Iris:* Iris recognition/matching is based upon the unique patterns in the colored ring in the eye that surrounds the pupil (see Figure B.1).* Collection is performed by a camera that takes a picture of the iris, which has been illuminated by a near-infrared device. Iris matching is considered much more accurate than fingerprint matching because there are many more points of comparison for irises than with fingerprints.† The power of the lens and the illuminating source determines the distance at which effective collection can be done, so increased power in both can offer greater standoff distance from collector to target, but not close to that available or

* Iris use is frequently confused with retina in media reporting. As the illustration above shows, the iris and the retina are on opposite sides of the eyeball. Retina matching uses the vein patterns at the back of the eye. Although retina collection and matching have been described as being used to control access to certain high security facilities, I have been unable to discover mention of any specific employments of retina technology.

† The Wikipedia page for iris recognition states that there are up to 200 points of comparison available. Fingerprint identification for law enforcement purposes is typically done with less than 15 minutiae points that match, although up to 50 points may match in good-quality fingerprint pairs.

potentially available with FR. Iris is also generally considered to be faster to match than fingerprints as well as more accurate, particularly in large-scale datasets, where the number of potential matches may be in the tens of millions. These advantages at least partially explain the growing worldwide use of iris identification/verification in immigration, homeland security, and access-control applications. The growing use of iris will also increase the potential availability of iris data that can be used to match, which may make it a more important modality for military applications in the future.

*DNA:* DNA is highly accurate and highly unique (with exception of maternal/identical multiples); however, using DNA for identification requires extensive and expensive training, technical processing, and infrastructure support. It also requires careful handling and preservation of the DNA sample (normally under temperature control) and is highly prone to sample contamination and/or degradation. Effective use for military operations will usually require the support of a deployed lab or similar capability, although a number of rapid DNA processing systems have recently been developed that have the potential to both make DNA more operationally useful and reduce some of the deployed infrastructure requirements (Figure B.2).

**Figure B.2** ISAF soldier in Afghanistan collects DNA via a cheek swab. DNA is a critical modality for intelligence purposes, but advanced capabilities for processing and matching are needed to make it more useful for combat identification.

*Voice:* Voice recognition is done by matching the pattern of one "voice print" to another. There are significant technical hurdles that need to be overcome to make it militarily useful. The most significant challenge is being able to collect a high-quality sample in an uncontrolled environment with background noise and to process it for matching. An individual's voice pattern is affected by biological factors such as the shape of the mouth and throat, which change as one ages, and it can also be affected by health factors such as having a cold or laryngitis. Voice is also normally classified as a behavioral modality, in that individuals can change the way they speak, particularly over time. These factors weaken the case for using voice pattern recognition for most military applications. However, the ability to collect voice samples remotely, covertly, or even forensically (e.g., from a recording) make this a modality that will see continued research and development, particularly from military intelligence organizations.

*Palm:* Collecting and matching palm prints is very similar to fingerprints, although the size of the palm surface requires a larger collection/imaging system, which rules out collection with a handheld system. U.S. forces in Iraq collected palm prints using the BISA base access system, but the prints themselves were not used for automated matching, because none of our systems then in use, including the DoD's ABIS, were capable of matching palm prints. Palm prints do have a great deal of utility from a latent/forensic standpoint, as they are often found on captured enemy equipment and documents or at locations of military or criminal activity. Most current biometric matching systems being marketed for law enforcement purposes advertise the ability to match on palm and "writer's palm" prints (Figure B.3).*

*Gait:* The manner in which one moves is both collectable and measurable. It is also thought to be fairly unique to each individual and thus a candidate for use in biometric matching. One of the attractive features of gait as a modality is the ability to capture it from a distance and potentially covertly using the same camera that one might employ for standoff facial recognition. There has also been some research into the use of gait to assess the intent of an individual. For example, if you collected repeated samples of a person's gait as he or she approached a base access point and then one day it appeared different, that might be an indicator that the individual is

* "Writer's palm" refers to the side of the hand. The latent impressions are frequently found on documents. Marines in Anbar Province in Iraq used to collect similar prints that they termed "knife edge" prints. These were used for manual latent matching, only not for automated matching, as previously mentioned.

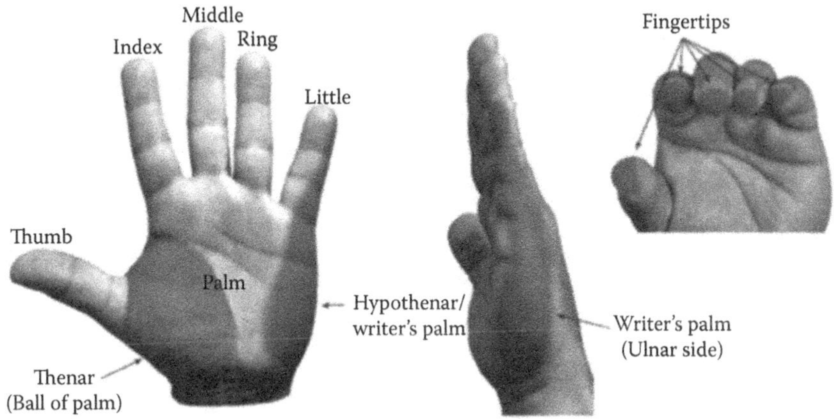


**Figure B.3** Key structures of the hand/palm.

carrying a weapon or wearing a suicide vest. At this point though, gait by itself is not really useful for military identification purposes.

*Other modalities:* There are certainly many other kinds of bodily measurements that can be used for identification or verification, and anyone who follows biometrics development cannot help but be amazed at some of the research into modalities like body odor, heat signature, or tears. While many of these will probably not have much application for military purposes, some of these lesser known modalities may offer the potential for more use, in conjunction with currently employed modalities, to provide improved accuracy. For example, ear lobe geometry could be used in conjunction with standoff facial recognition to increase matching accuracy and to allow more definitive matching from partial or off-angle facial images (assuming the ear is visible, of course). Others could be incorporated into biometric sensors to improve the accuracy and better detect spoofing attempts, such as adding vein capture capability to a fingerprint sensor.

## COMPARING BIOMETRIC MODALITIES (TABLE B.2)

In Chapter 1, I briefly discussed some of the factors used to compare biometric modalities. Here is a more complete list with explanations of each:

*Universality:* This factor is concerned with how universal a type of biometric is within the target population. Before you say "well, everyone has fingers", consider a population of rural people who

**Table B.2** Modality Comparison Chart

| Modality | Universality | Uniqueness | Permanence | Collectability | Performance | Acceptability | Circumvention |
|---|---|---|---|---|---|---|---|
| Face | H | M | M | H | M | H | H |
| Finger | M | H | M | M | H | H | M |
| Gait | H | M | M | H | L | M | M |
| Iris | H | H | H | H | H | M | L |
| Retina | H | H | H | M | H | L | L |
| DNA | H | H | H | L | H | L | L |
| Voice | M | H | L | M | M | H | H |

*Source:* This table came from a research paper published by the *International Journal of Advanced Research in Computer Science and Software Engineering* in April 2014 (Volume 4, Issue 4, ISSN: 2277 128X). I only included those modalities with the greatest military applications.

*Note:* The ratings here are representative of those I have seen on a number of similar charts; however, I don't agree with all of them. For example, regarding DNA, I agree that it *is* extremely hard (or maybe impossible) to spoof a properly collected DNA sample taken directly from an individual; it is relatively easy to leave a false sample at a crime scene. A DNA sample can also be corrupted by improper collection, processing or storage procedures, as has been previously noted. H = high, M = medium, and L = low.

work with their hands doing farming or other manual labor. Some of them are going to lose fingers in accidents and some may have their fingerprints so worn down or obscured by scars that collecting a usable print might be difficult or impossible.

*Uniqueness:* Research indicates that not all modalities are as measurably unique in one population set as compared to another. For example in populations with little ethnic diversity, there might be less variance in facial features making face potentially a less useful modality.

*Permanence:* Many measurable human features will change over time as a person grows and gets older. This is particularly true of facial features, and hand geometry in particular. This factor could negatively affect the use of certain modalities for long-term identification or verification applications.

*Collectability:* The ease or difficulty of collecting a biometric sample will differ for each modality. It is much easier and less time-consuming to take a picture of a person's face than to collect ten fingerprints, whether slaps or rolls. Although this is not usually a consideration from an academic perspective, obviously equipment availability will have a significant impact on this factor in practical/operational terms.

*Performance:* The relative speed and accuracy of the matching process will also differ according to the modality. Of course, one's technical capabilities will obviously have a major impact on this factor as well. Better equipment and more powerful algorithms can overcome some of the relative performance weaknesses.

*Acceptability:* The use of some modalities may be greatly affected by the cultural or legal environment, such as the cultural prohibition of women showing their faces in public in some of the most conservative Muslim societies. On the other hand, people around the world have the heebie jeebies about having their DNA collected, particularly if it is done in an overt and invasive manner such as with a cheek (buccal) swab.

*Circumvention:* This factor deals with the relative ability of a particular modality to be spoofed (employing a forged or fraudulent sample such as a fake finger) or bypassed. Once again, the technical or procedural aspects will determine how this works in the real world. For example, a fingerprint scanner may be able to be fooled by a fake finger device, but that will not matter if collection is done directly or is observed.

# APPENDIX C: COMMON BIOMETRICS SYSTEMS AND DESIRED FEATURES

Although I have downplayed the criticality of biometrics systems when compared to the development of concepts of employment and adequate Tactics, Techniques and Procedures (TTPs) and the proper planning and preparation for their usage, it is still necessary to have a brief discussion of the most commonly used systems. While I'll point out some of the more relevant features (or features that are lacking), I won't provide a comprehensive list of specifications that are available from many other sources, including the websites of the companies that make the systems. I will also refrain from picking sides by evaluating one system against the other, which is beyond my personal knowledge and expertise and could negatively impact my future job prospects. The only exception to this is with regard to the BAT and HIIDE systems for which I have more personal knowledge.

## DESIRED SYSTEM FEATURES FOR COLLECTION DEVICES

Biometrics collection systems come in all shapes and sizes, and with differences in functionality that are based, to a certain extent, upon the kinds of missions they are designed support. I say "to a certain extent," because I'm not sure most vendors of handheld systems really think beyond the sort of generic, direct multimodal biometric collection typified by a soldier on patrol collecting biometrics from a suspected enemy. As I've described in this book, there are many ways that biometrics can be used in military operations; thus, there cannot be a "one size fits all" approach to system design. Here are some of the key areas that developers of military biometric collection systems need to consider.

- *Modalities:* Most of the handheld collection systems offered for potential military use are multimodal systems that collect fingerprints, facial photos and iris images. Some system vendors will also claim that their models collect latent prints, although I suspect, some qualifications may be in order here. While multimodal systems are certainly welcome, I think there is probably some risk that they may not be maximized for any one particular modality. In fact, there may be good reasons to employ a system that is not multimodal for certain kinds of missions. For example, recalling the issue with the Marines in Helmand Province, Afghanistan, which I discussed in Chapter 3, it may make sense for a military force to deploy an iris-only collection device like the Pier, if they are using it for population management purposes only. Other uses of a unimodal system could be for detainee management or to screen locally hired personnel for base access purposes. The main point here is that a system that collects only a single modality may be adequate for use as a verification tool with a relatively stable population set, AFTER a full enrollment has taken place. Moreover, using a simpler and less expensive single modality device may make it more likely to be actually used, and will free up the multimodal systems for identification missions.

- *Form factor:* When it comes to handheld systems, all things being equal, the smaller and lighter, the better. The usual descriptor here is "cargo packet" capable. In other words, can it fit in the cargo pocket of the pants in a tactical uniform? This has naturally led developers down the path of a cellphone-like system. Unfortunately, all things are not equal, and there are undoubtedly tradeoffs in performance from a system that you cannot only hold *with your hands* but hold *in your hand*. For example, taking a photo of a face or iris in a bright sunlight environment, or collecting multiple fingerprints at one time, is going to be a challenge with a cellphone-type device. One possible solution would be to design such systems to be used with accessories or plug-in peripherals that could maximize the collection of certain modalities in certain conditions, and that would expand the range of missions the system can support. For example, a system could come with a binocular-like accessory with which it could be docked to maximize the collection of iris images (similar to the concept behind the Trident system I describe below). Or for static missions, the system could be connected to a full-size, ten-finger collection device to both speed the collection of fingerprints (and perhaps palm prints), during full enrollments and ensure the highest quality of print capture.

- *Versatility/flexibility (all-in-one, system-of-systems, mission apps):* The handheld collection systems being developed today are largely designed to be employed in a stand-alone fashion for a maximum variety of missions. My above concerns notwithstanding, this is a valid approach and certainly is the one being favored by the DoD. But what if, instead, a system was built using a single hub that held the core functionality (database, matching, communication), while the actual collections were done by a variety of purpose-built sensors that fed their data to the central hub for local matching and sharing via an encrypted local Wi-Fi network for similar technology? An approach like this might allow for a wider proliferation of simpler and cheaper biometric sensors across a force linked to only a few of the more complex and expensive hub devices. Such a system-of-systems (or biometrics network) approach might make sense in static situations, or even for mobile operations using tactical vehicles, where the hub could be mounted in one of the vehicles. Only those forces operating completely on foot and out of range of a hub would actually need a multimodal handheld system.

  Another approach that could enhance the versatility and functionality of even the most complex all-in-one system, would be the ability to download (or create) mission-specific apps and, perhaps, mission-specific algorithms. This concept is similar to one that was first developed by folks on the staff of PM Biometrics (in particular, Larry Campbell), as well as the team of requirements developers out of Ft. Huachuca, Arizona, whose efforts I managed when I was the requirements lead at the Biometrics Task Force. The idea then was that rather than focusing on biometrics hardware *and*_software development, the DoD would just focus on building a collection of biometric software modules, which could be downloaded onto a variety of preapproved commercially developed hardware platforms. This software could be tailored to certain kinds of devices or certain kinds of missions. For example, if you were going to do an iris-based verification mission with your devices, you would download and install the appropriate (and updated) software for your devices prior to the mission.

Although, this concept did not gain the favor of my BTF leadership at the time, I believe it was a sound one and is even more so today, using Android-based cellphone technology. So, say you want to do an iris collection mission—we've got an App for that. Apps could even be built to support specific types of missions which could replicate the kind of on-the-fly/overnight development efforts that the early developers of the BAT folks often had to do. So now, if you have recently begun a major combat operation and need to manage a growing detainee populace, you download the appropriate App, which includes the various forms you need to accomplish your mission. Are you doing site exploitation? You can download a suite of Apps that includes everything from latent-print capture, to digitizing and reporting images of captured enemy documents and equipment. And, if your always-inventive soldiers find a new way to support a new mission using biometrics, they can design their own Apps and post them to the Identity Apps Store.

- *Variable matching algorithms and threshold settings:* Here is where my limited technical capacity may get me into some trouble, but I am going to strike out anyway, and state my belief that it might be desirable to have "tunable" biometrics systems that could allow an operator to select system sensitivity based upon the mission and threat circumstances. "Sensitivity" may not be the right term, but what I am envisioning is that it could be possible to use a variable combination of algorithms, including the use of multialgorithm fusion, and threshold settings, to either provide the maximum assurance and accuracy of the match result, or to speed the match process in a high-throughput/low-threat situation. So in a base-access situation, where there are lots of people we need to process and the threat is relatively low, we might be willing to allow a higher FAR (False Acceptance Rate) in the interests of speed and efficiency with our base-access process. If in another instance, we have detected threats to our base, we might put our base-access biometrics system on the "High Threat" setting, which would both increase the match threshold score *and* employ a slower but more accurate matching algorithm or use multialgorithm fusion. In this case, we are willing to cause back-ups at the gate and delay the entry of our local workforce in the interest of maximizing base security.

- *Data input (pull-down menus, prefillable screens, embedded GPS):* From an ease-of-use perspective, anything that makes it simpler and faster to input data, is going to be popular with the military user. On the other hand, from the perspective of a biometrics database manager or intelligence analyst, anything that makes it easier to not put in data is a problem. For example, pull-down menus that allow a system operator to choose from preselected values may speed the time required to complete an enrollment, but they can also result in a lack of precision, which could be a problem later on, when we are analyzing the data for intelligence purposes or using it to enhance the matching purposes.* From this perspective, a system needs to allow for both generalized data entry via pull-down or preselected values, *or* the ability to manually input specific information dependent upon the military situation.

  One data element input that absolutely needs to be as automated as possible is geolocational data. The BAT/HIIDE systems in use in Afghanistan when I was there did not have an embedded GPS function and thus required system users to manually input the locations of each enrollment, which they frequently failed to do. Not having such information seriously weakens the value of the enrollment data for subsequent intelligence or operational purposes, since I can't go capture someone if I don't know where the individual is or was. It would be further helpful for the system to allow for data to be prepopulated, so if an enrollment mission is being planned in a specific town or village at a particular time, fields such as date, enrolling unit, name of location, reason for enrollment, and such can be filled out *before* the mission begins, greatly reducing the time needed to complete the enrollments. Flexibility is the key with these kinds of features, as the actual use should be dictated by the mission, circumstances, and local policy, not by the system.
- *Quality management:* Being able to get immediate feedback on the quality of the biometric sample while it is being collected is a desirable key feature for biometric collection systems. Such a

* For example, if I am recording an individual's biological characteristics, such as height and age, the system is likely to have a range of preselected options from which to choose. This feature will make it faster to input the data, but the data will also lack specificity. This lack of specificity could have negative impact if I am trying to use this biological/"soft biometric" data for the kind of advanced matching process described in the Afterword.

feature could have a major impact on the quality of our biometrics databases, which tend to function on the GIGO (Garbage In, Garbage Out) principle. It could also help reduce the time and resources that are required to do manual file processing and matching. However, there have to be over rides to allow for data collection when conditions make high-quality capture difficult, such as when someone is shooting at you. Perhaps there could also be a switch to allow the operator to dumb-down or shut off the quality check feature if necessary. The GIGO principle notwithstanding, I'm a firm believer that some data, even less than perfect data, are better than no data, even if they may have to be segregated within the database.

- *Communications:* I have frequently described the communications challenges that have bedeviled our biometrics operations over the past decade. The inability of the HIIDE to transmit data without being connected to a BAT was especially problematic in Afghanistan, where the United States and its allies performed more foot-mobile missions away from the FOBs where the BAT systems tended to be located. Thus, soldiers could be out for days doing biometric collections that they could not transmit back to the ABIS and using BEWLs that they could not update. Various solutions to this problem were researched, and some field-tested, including the establishment of field deployable 3G/4G cellular networks as well as attempts to pass biometrics data via tactical radios.

  More modern biometric devices, such as the SEEK systems, are not only able to send and receive data autonomously, they are able to interface directly with a wide variety of communications systems, such as the portable tactical satellite terminals used by U.S. SOF. While direct submission of biometric data via dedicated satellite communications may not be feasible for future large-scale conventional military operations, it may be possible for the kinds of smaller-scale and shorter-duration operations that are likely to be predominant in the postwar/interwar period.

  A number of the more recently developed systems, particularly those such as the Trident system described below, are based on Android cellular-phone technology and share the Bluetooth capability that modern cellphones possess. With this capability for local communications, it might be possible for the individual collection devices being used during an operation to share data as it is being collected, which could provide expanded opportunities for local matching using the data held in all the systems, not just the one doing the actual collection. In addition, if these handheld devices are able to collect and share latent prints, it might be possible for one element in an operation to match latent prints collected off captured enemy material to direct collections from suspects being taken elsewhere in the operational area. Local Wi-Fi communications might also make it possible to share data using the collector-and-hub system I described previously. The larger hub could hold an expanded watchlist, or even part of the DoD central database, and could possibly perform expanded local matching. It could also serve as the means for communicating these collections back to the central database via satellite, or some other tactical communications system.

## CURRENT COLLECTIONS SYSTEMS

There are a quite a number of collection systems that have been developed over the past decade, with or without some government development effort (i.e., Commercial off-the-Shelf/COTS or Government off-the-Shelf/GOTS). I will focus on the relatively few that have seen fairly widespread use in Iraq, Afghanistan, or elsewhere, in support of the U.S. military's worldwide counterterrorism/counterinsurgency efforts. These include the BAT/HIIDE system, the SEEK family of systems, the Cogent Fusions systems, the Pier, and a few others that may not be in current military use, but which appear to have potential applications.

Current biometric collection systems have been developed for use in a static setting or configured to be carried by soldiers into the field. These are capable of collecting a single type of modality or may be able to collect multiple modalities. Some systems are entirely self-contained/all-in-one devices, while others are capable of interfacing with a wide variety of peripheral devices (e.g., fingerprint scanners, iris capture devices, cameras, or printers). Some can be used in a stand-alone/untethered manner, while others must be plugged into a computer or another kind of biometrics device, in order to upload or download data. Most devices have the ability to perform an immediate comparison between a newly collected biometric file and one that was previously collected and stored on the system, but others are also capable of uploading a biometric watchlist against which newly collected biometrics can also be matched. The amount of storage space available on each varies widely. Some have the ability to perform noncollection but related tasks such as printing biometrically-enabled ID/access cards.

*BAT/HIIDE: The Aging and Somewhat Infirm King and Queen of the Biometrics Battlefield*

I mentioned some of the downsides of the BAT/HIIDE system in Chapter 2, but it is important to note that the system was deployed widely in Iraq and Afghanistan and that users of the BAT and HIIDE included personnel from organizations outside of the U.S. Army, including members of other services and foreign partners. In fact, with regard to the various operators of the system, the BAT/HIIDE is both a joint and combined biometrics system. Further, the inability of the U.S. Army or the Joint Force to fund and develop a truly joint replacement means that these systems are likely to continue to be used at least in some capacity for the foreseeable future.

We discussed some of the negatives of the BAT and HIIDE previously; so what are the positives? First, the BAT is a very flexible system that can be employed in support of a wide range of missions. This is partly due to the nature of the system, which is, at its core, simply a ruggedized laptop computer. Like any computer, you can upload a wide variety of software to run the peripheral devices used to collect biometrics, and it can be modified to incorporate functions specific to various military missions, such as base access, detainee management, and so forth. The peripheral devices include different kinds of fingerprint capture systems, from those that collect one flat print at a time to those that can collect an entire hand print and rolled prints as well. Various iris capture devices can also be used, as well as a variety of cameras for the capture of facial images. As any computer, the BAT system can be hooked up to various kinds of networks, which, in the military, means that it can be run on unclassified or classified networks. With the right kind of printer and software, a BAT can print badges, making the system suitable (if not optimal) for use as a base-access control system, which was a key mission supported by BATs in Afghanistan. Moreover, since it is a laptop, storage space is normally much more robust than is the case with a handheld system like the HIIDE or SEEK. As typically configured, BATs can also be used for tactical missions if the collection activities are performed in a static location with access to a commercial power source. However, as I described in Chapter 2, the BAT is not suitable for "field usage," unless significant nonstandard modifications of the type done by TF Biometrics in Afghanistan are made.

One of the key capabilities of the BAT software is the ability to create and manage identity profiles for intelligence purposes, which was the original purpose of the system. A BAT "dossier" on an individual identity can include much more information than a typical enrollment file, including intelligence reports or analyses, relevant forensics reports, or other identity information collected by nonbiometric devices, such as standard photos. The robustness of these BAT dossiers allows a significant amount of information to be available to a BAT operator anywhere within the network; however, all that data comes with a price in terms of communications bandwidth requirements and data latency problems.

The HIIDE device was originally developed as a separate system from the BAT (it was an outgrowth of the original Pier iris capture and matching system); however, it was designed to plug into and sync with a BAT, in order to send and receive data. The HIIDE has certain tactical advantages in that it is a totally self-contained system capable of collected flat fingerprints (one at a time), iris images, and facial photos, without any additional equipment. It is also a fairly small and relatively light device, although not quite "cargo pocket capable." Other than its inability to send or receive data autonomously, the HIIDE also suffers from a number of other limitations, including the lack of a rolled print capability, and the fact that it is very difficult to capture iris images in bright light situations. The enrollment process is also slowed by the small fingerprint sensor (which allows one print to be collected at a time), and there is no way to prepopulate any of the required enrollment data fields, nor is there an embedded GPS feature, which would allow critical locational data to be automatically added. The result is that soldiers in less secure environments are sometimes hesitant to do full enrollments, which could take up to 15 min each and would often leave out important information, including the geographic data, which could be critical for subsequent intelligence analysis. But, the HIIDE is fairly simple to use and that fact, along with its widespread deployment, makes it an important collection system.

*Guardian Jump Kit*: The suitcase-enclosed Crossmatch Guardian Jump Kit was one of the earlier mobile multimodel systems. It is not a handheld, self-contained system like the HIIDE or SEEK systems but is comparable to the BAT in that it is based on a small laptop computer with attached peripheral collections devices allowing it to collect and match face, finger, and iris. Because it is laptop-based, the system is very flexible and configurable like a BAT and can incorporate a wide variety of optional devices, including a printer, document scanner, and latent image capture device, assembled into a large waterproof case; it often weighs more than 30 pounds (Figure C.1).

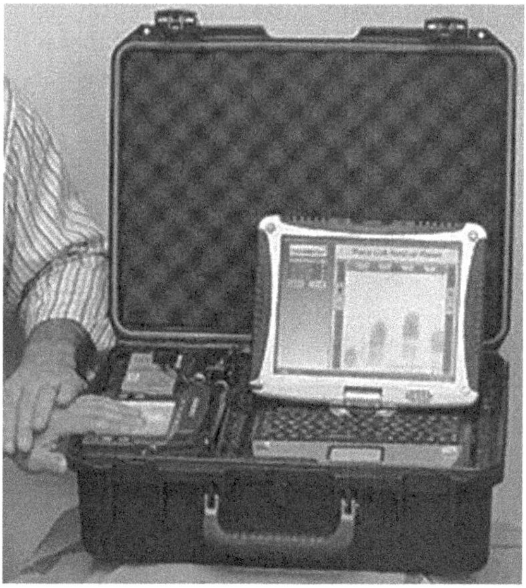

**Figure C.1** The Crossmatch Jump Kit was an early biometric collection device with similar features as the BAT.

## MANY OPERATORS SEEK THE FEATURES FOUND IN THE SEEK FAMILY OF DEVICES

The original Crossmatch Secure Electronic Enrollment Kit (SEEK) was first launched in early 2009, and contained an embedded PC running Crossmatch MOBS SW along with a 1.3 MP camera, a dual iris capture device, a dual fingerprint/roll capture device, a 4" touch display, a 60,000-person on-board watchlist capability, 3G communication and a six-hour battery, which were all contained in a four-pound package. After initial deployments in 2009, we began working with the U.S. military on an improved model based upon feedback received from multiple agencies. In early 2010, the SEEK® II model was launched, which added a full keyboard, rugged display and port covers, and one-handed support mounts. This device was approved for deployment across all U.S. military agencies, for both enrollment of unknown persons into authoritative databases and verification against both the internal watchlist and the external authoritative databases. Thousands of devices are still being used worldwide and SEEK® II has become the standard for mobile multibiometric enrollment devices.

SEEK devices replaced the Jumpkits and Cogent devices in the 2009-2010 period as the system of choice for U.S. Special Forces due to their compact design and speed of operation.

*Cogent Fusion* (L-1/Morpho): The Fusion device is one of the lightest (in terms of weight, just over a pound), multimodal systems on the market, able to capture and store 100,000-plus (scalable) records: forensic quality fingerprints, latent fingerprints, iris images, photos, and textual data. Other optional capabilities include: searching and matching against internally-stored biometric records; 360° latent print searching; 3G wireless connectivity, cellular radio, or Bluetooth; and GPS tagging of all records collected. But because it lacks the ability to upload a biometrics watchlist, it is probably not suitable for disconnected (i.e., without direct communications to a database) military operations. The first devices were sold to DoD via the REF in June 2008, with follow-on orders over the next two or three years that totalled 1,000(+) (Figure C.2).

*Pier:* The Pier device was originally designed by a small company called Securimetrics to provide the BAT with a means to collect and match iris images. Various models were subsequently developed some for stand-alone use, which was popular with the U.S. Marine Corps in Anbar

**Figure C.2** The Cogent Fusion devices are capable systems, but the inability of the versions provided to the Afghan government to upload and match against a watchlist caused some problems for ISAF.

Province, Iraq. The Pier was also the basis for DoD's original handheld multimodal collections and matching the system, the HIIDE.

*New Collection Systems:* Various companies are continuing to develop handheld collections systems, many based upon a cellphone- or tablet-like device. One company that has taken a different approach is Credence ID, whose Trident handheld looks like an overgrown pair of binoculars and is designed to maximize the collection of iris images. Although it has not yet seen military action, the Trident is in use in a number of countries and international agencies that are focusing on the use of iris as a population and resource management tool. The Indonesian government is using the Trident for law enforcement purposes across the hundreds of islands that make up that archipelago-like nation. Many of the operations are very similar to those conducted in a military environment (Figure C.3).

*Database/matching Systems:* Biometric databases and matching systems are becoming more prevalent across the world, as countries increase their employment of biometrics in areas such as law enforcement and immigration/border control. Most of these systems can be categorized as either an Automated Fingerprint Identification System (AFIS) or an Automated Biometric Identification System (ABIS). An AFIS or ABIS generally functions the same way, although the latter is typically distinguished by the ability to employ more than one biometric modality. An AFIS/ABIS

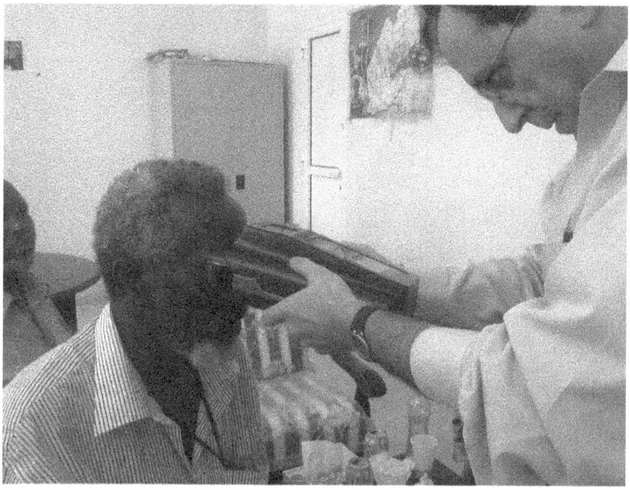

**Figure C.3** Many of the new biometric collections systems, such as the Credence ID Trident, are based upon Android cellular technology.

will maintain a core database of enrollment files, which include biometric collections on particular individuals, as well as varying amounts of additional textual information, including biographical information and information regarding the circumstances of each biometric collection (*aka* "contextual data"). Separate algorithms are included for matching the various kinds of modalities included in the systems. Unidentified latent print images are normally kept in a separate but linked data store (often referred to as an Unmatched Latent File or ULF). New live or latent collections will be submitted to the system and compared to all existing biometric files, and an automated "match"/"no match"/"possible match" result will be reported.* The results will then be reported to the submitter of the newly collected data, generally through a separate communication means.†

*DoD Automated Biometric Identification System (ABIS):* In 2004, the Army's Biometrics Fusion Center (BFC) established the DoD ABIS to assist in the Global War on Terrorism (GWoT). Developed as a prototype based on the FBI's Integrated Automated Fingerprint Identification System (IAFIS), ABIS' initial mission was to use fingerprint data as a method of establishing positive identification of known or suspected terrorists, and for screening individuals before granting them privileges associated with positions of trust. The prototype ABIS was developed by leveraging the technology (and actual hardware) used by the FBI IAFIS system. Additional modalities, including face, iris, and palm, were added over the ensuing years, and multimodal fusion capability was incorporated in 2009. The DoD currently has plans to field an advanced replacement system, which will be known as the BEC (Biometrics Enabling Capability) when fielded.

*Biometric Access Control Systems:* There has only been one biometric base access control/screening system specifically designed for deployed military forces—the BISA (Biometrics Identification System for Access) described below. In many cases, a collection system like the BAT, or even handheld systems like the HIIDE or SEEK, can function as a screening device on smaller facilities or on a temporary basis, but there are certain

* Latent print matches, and sometimes facial recognition matches, will return a list of possible matched pairs known as a candidate list, which will then be reviewed and a final match decision made by trained human examiners.

† Collectors and submitters of biometrics collections will typically not have direct access to a biometrics database, and thus the match results will have to be sent to them via some kind of communications means, including posting to a website, a specially formatted message, or via a radio or phone notification.

advantages to a system designed specifically for the base-access role. All such systems need to be able to collect, store, and locally match biometrics, preferably using at least fingerprint (for initial identification and verification) and iris (for recurring verification) modalities. They need communications connectivity to the larger regional or strategic biometric database for the initial vetting of newly enrolled local employees and visitors and for receiving updated watchlist information. The system must also be able to share data rapidly with other base access systems in the operational area and with tactical forces conducting biometric collections during combat and combat-related operations. Finally, the ability to print biometric access badges and scan them at access points should be a standard feature for long-term use at larger facilities.

*Biometrics Identification System for Access:* BISA was produced by a rapid development effort in late 2004, after the Mosul Dining Facility (DFAC) bombing described in Chapter 1.* The Tier 1 system was deployed in 2005 and fielded at the 10 largest facilities in Iraq. It was followed by the Tier 2 system, which was established at smaller bases in Iraq as well as in Kuwait. The BISA system provided the means to biometrically register, vet, and screen workers and visitors to Coalition facilities in Iraq. The Tier 1 version was a completely self-contained capability that included workstations, power generation, and satellite communities packed into and operated from two large shipping containers. This version required significant site preparation, which could only be accomplished at larger facilities, so Tier 2, a scaled-down version with less hardware, was developed and used at the smaller facilities in Iraq. Both versions incorporated a handheld device for use at access gates to quickly scan the biometric badges and do a 1:1 comparison between the biometrics stored on the card and a live collection for those issued badges. The U.S. Army eventually decided not to acquire BISA for use outside of Iraq, and the system is now operating only at the remaining few U.S. facilities in the country by the U.S. State Department, including the U.S. Embassy in Baghdad.†

*Defense Biometrics Identification System:* There is currently no joint service biometrics access control system, and most DoD facilities do not use biometrics. However, the U.S. Air Force acquired the DBIDS (Defense Biometrics Identification System) for use at joint bases and other facilities

* The system development was led by the Director of the Biometrics Fusion Center under a mandate from the Joint Staff J-34 in the Pentagon.

† Given the large number of forces we have deployed around the world, the DoD's failure to acquire a dedicated deployable biometrics access control capability is a serious mistake.

that it controls, including those in the United States, in Europe, at various locations in Southwest Asia, and in Asia (including South Korea, where it was initially installed in the late 1990s). Calling it an "identification" system it is a bit of a misnomer, since it is actually intended to simply verify the identities of individuals who have already been identified and vetted, and who require recurring access to a base. Most of those registered in DBIDS are DoD civilian employees, military, family members, and some contractors, who have been issued a Common Access Card by the Defense Manpower Data Center (DMDC). For those non-CAC holders, such as many contractors and recurring visitors, nonbiometrics background checks are done according to base procedures, usually by the base security organization, and the individual is registered in DBIDS and issued an access card. Upon an individual entering a base, the system is used to verify that the person's CAC is legitimate and still active and that there is no derogatory information associated with the card holder (such as a DUI). It can also be used to biometrically verify the individual as he/she enters the facility, based upon the threat condition and base commander guidance.

## BIOMETRIC INTELLIGENCE SYSTEMS

The Biometrics Identity Management Agency Biometrics Glossary defines Biometrics-Enabled Intelligence (BEI) as "Intelligence resulting from the collection, processing, analysis, and interpretation of biometric signatures; the contextual data associated with those signatures; and other available intelligence that answers a commander's or other decision-maker's information needs concerning persons, networks, or populations of interest." The BAT system was designed as much for intelligence purposes as for biometric collection and that it incorporated its own intelligence capability within the system's software. This allowed for the creation of dossiers and the sharing of this data, as well as subsequent changes and additions to the dossiers, with anyone on the BAT network.*

The BAT's combination of collection and intelligence functionality is unique for military biometrics systems. For those not on the BAT network,

* This was a great capability and allowed the BAT to operate fairly effectively independent of a larger database, as it did during initial deployment in the Balkans. However, it also caused significant problems when the communication network that tied these BAT systems together was not robust enough to move all of this data in a timely manner, which was often the case.

and particularly with regard to the strategic database ABIS, separate intelligence analytical systems had to be developed in order to perform the BEI and identity intelligence functions that are so critical to making biometrics relevant for military operations. In Chapter 9, I discussed my thoughts on the DoD's future biometrics enterprise and why I believe that the next generations of our strategic capability need to combine the biometrics and intelligence functions into a single system. However, that is not how we have operated over the past decade—for three principle reasons. One, performing intelligence analysis and operational functions, like operating the ABIS database, are executed by separate parts of the U.S. military, and there is little precedence yet for fully integrated intelligence and operational systems. Two, the design of the ABIS did not include any analytical functionality beyond that needed to perform the biometrics matching function. And three, the U.S. ABIS system operates on an unclassified network, with an unclassified database, while most intelligence systems and functions operate on classified networks.

# APPENDIX D: ORGANIZING BIOMETRICS FOR COMBAT

Given the absence of formal biometrics doctrine within DoD (Department of Defense), as I've previously mentioned, it should not be surprising that there is no agreed-upon formula on how to organize for biometrics missions. Different organizational approaches to biometrics exist at the service levels, at the Combatant Command level, and in the theaters of operations (Iraq vs. Afghanistan). To a large extent, these differences mirror the split between those who view biometrics as an operational tool versus those that consider biometrics more of an intelligence tool, which I have noted earlier. Overall, the preponderance of biometric activity across the DoD is driven more by intelligence-related organizations, than by those elements with an operational focus, particularly with respect to biometric activities outside of Afghanistan.

The organizations described below are those that are specifically and principally focused on biometrics or identity functions. There are other organizations that may do some biometrics work, in addition to other tasks, as well as individuals who perform some biometric functions in organizations, who may or may not have biometrics in their job descriptions. Across the services, there are no formal military occupational specialties for biometrics, although there some civilian positions in various organizational structures that include "biometrics" in their job titles. Military personnel in biometric organizations are normally those assigned from other specialty areas, such as intelligence, military police, or others.

## THE SERVICES

The Army has been the leader in biometrics since the beginning of DoD's involvement with the technology. My former organization, the Biometrics and Identity Management Agency (BIMA, now known as the Defense Forensics and Biometrics Agency or DFBA), began as two separate organizations under the communications staff element (CIO/G6) at the U.S. Army headquarters. One of these organizations, the Biometrics Fusion Center (BFC), operated the then nascent DoD biometrics database out of offices in West Virginia, while a policy and planning organization called the Biometrics Management Office (BMO) operated in the DC area. In 2007, the two organizations were merged, designated as the Biometrics Task Force (BTF), and brought under the Army Chief of Staff for Operations (G-3/5/7) in recognition of the increasing role of biometrics in supporting combat operations in Iraq and Afghanistan. The following year, the Department of Defense issued a DoD Directive (DoDD) designating the U.S. Army as the "Executive Agent" for DoD biometrics, with responsibility for operating the DoD's ABIS and for developing biometrics policies and procedures on the behalf of the entire Defense Department.

DoDD 8521–01E also charged the Army with the responsibility for the acquisition and technical development of the most "common" DoD biometrics systems, through the establishment of a Program Manager (PM) for DoD Biometrics. The PM office (commonly called "PM Biometrics") was initially created in 2007 and gradually assumed responsibility for most of the DoD's tactical collection systems, the BISA base-access system, and the development of the ABIS. Despite not being designated as a joint program office, PM Biometrics has attempted to meet the needs of all the services while, at the same time, providing direct support to biometrics operations in Iraq and Afghanistan (more on that shortly).

In addition to the BIMA/DFBA and PM Bio, the Army's intelligence elements have been very active in biometrics and can rightly claim to have been responsible for developing the original tactical biometrics collections systems: BAT and HIIDE. The Army Chief of Staff for Intelligence (G2) maintains a small staff responsible for overseeing a number of intelligence-related biometrics programs and research projects, while the Army's Intelligence and Security Command and its subordinate and previously mentioned National Ground Intelligence Center (NGIC) have focused more on biometrics-related intelligence analysis and production. Another key player on the intelligence side has been the TRADOC* Capability Manager for Biometric and Forensics, which operates out of Fort Huachuca, Arizona, and is intended to represent the Army's interest in the development of biometrics capabilities, doctrine, and procedures, which has brought it into frequent conflict with both the BIMA/DFBA and PM Biometrics.

* The U.S. Army's Training and Doctrine Command (TRADOC) is responsible for overseeing training organizations and facilities, establishing operational doctrine and procedures, and developing and documenting operational requirements for Army combat and supporting systems.

Because there is no formal, institutional approach to biometrics in the Army, there are no formal biometrics positions within the Service's tactical force structure. Within higher headquarters (Division level and above), biometrics and forensics normally fall under an officer on the intelligence staff responsible for intelligence exploitation activities (e.g., G2X or J2X if in a joint organization), which often include a range of activities related to biometrics, forensics, and counter-IED. Below that level, Army biometrics tend to be treated as predominantly an intelligence concern and, thus, responsibility typically falls to the intelligence staffs at the Brigade level and below. A few years ago, the Army G2 was developing a concept for expanding intelligence support throughout the tactical force structure to include the establishment of intelligence support teams at least as far down as the company level. These teams, called "Company Intelligence Support Teams (COIST)," would have included biometrics and forensics capabilities; however, it is my understanding that this concept has been largely shelved and that currently there are no plans to field biometrics collection systems within the army's tactical force structure.

Given the similarities between the land-based missions performed by the Army and the Marines, you might believe that they would have the same approaches to biometrics and, to some extent, they do. However, the Marines were actually the first service to purchase large quantities of biometrics equipment, the first to develop and codify biometrics operating procedures during the earliest days of the Iraq war, the first service to conduct widespread training of their troops in biometrics operations, and the only service to have developed a service-wide operational concept for identity. The Marine Corps' policies and procedures for the use of biometrics are developed by its Identity Operation Section, which is part of the USMC (U.S. Marine Corps) Headquarters Plans, Policies and Operations Directorate. In 2011, the USMC published an Identity Operations Strategy, which was designed to be a coordinated and synchronized expeditionary Identity Operations capability to support identity dominance across the full "Range of Military Operations." The Marine Corps biometric-related intelligence issues are handled by a small office under the intelligence staff of HQ Marine Corps, which is developing identity intelligence strategy, policy and procedures to support future Marine expeditionary operations. One unique aspect of the Marine Corps approach is the linkage between biometrics/identity intelligence and law enforcement, an outgrowth of its experience in facilitating the prosecution of Iraq insurgents in Al Anbar Province.

The U.S. Air Force and U.S. Navy biometrics activities are on a much a smaller scale than that of either the Army or Marines, and neither has an organization solely dedicated to biometric operations. The U.S. Navy has a small Identity Intelligence office in the Office of Naval Intelligence and has used biometrics for selected maritime interdiction operations. The U.S. Air Force's interest in biometrics has largely been for base-access purposes.

## COMBATANT COMMANDS

One of the COCOMs with the greatest focus on biometrics is the U.S. Central Command (CENTCOM). Biometrics within the CENTCOM Headquarters has largely been dominated by the Operations Staff (J3), which includes an office responsible for biometrics and forensics within the division that covers force protection issues for the command. This arrangement makes some sense, since CENTCOM HQ does not have a great deal of control over day-to-day combat operations in Afghanistan (or Iraq previously), but it does have responsibility for the protection of U.S. forces and facilities throughout most of the Middle East. The support it does provide to biometrics operations in the combat zones tends to be more focused on helping acquire biometric systems for deployed forces, developing data-sharing agreements, and managing the data flow. Interestingly, while SOCOM and the other COCOMs view biometrics much more from an intelligence perspective, the direct involvement of the CENTCOM intelligence staff (J2) directorate has been fairly limited over the past decade.

The next most biometrically active COCOM is the U.S. Africa Command (AFRICOM), where the lead for biometrics is in the J2, but the overall effort is a shared responsibility of the intelligence and operations staffs. The AFRICOM biometrics program is called Identity Resolution and is heavily focused on engagements and data exchanges with partner nations in the AFRICOM Area of Responsibility and with building partner-nation capabilities. Of the remaining overseas-focused COCOMs, there are small but active biometrics or identity intelligence offices present within the J2 staffs of the U.S. Southern Command and the U.S. European Command, while the U.S. Pacific Command had only one or two individuals performing biometrics functions during my time at BIMA.

## ORGANIZATIONAL APPROACHES IN THE COMBAT THEATERS

Given the absence of any authoritative guidance on the employment of biometrics in combat and the somewhat differing organizational approaches at the service and COCOM levels, it is probably not surprising that command and control of biometrics also differed between Iraq and Afghanistan. In Iraq, biometrics capabilities were initially deployed by individual units with little centralized control or support. In 2007, the newly created PM DoD Biometrics funded the establishment of an organization in Iraq to provide support to the growing biometrics operations there. This office, known as PM Biometrics Forward (or more often, PM Forward), was headed initially by Colonel Natalie Jacaruso, who reported directly to the Chief of PM DoD Biometrics back in the U.S. as well as to senior Coalition military officials in Iraq. PM Forward involved a few military and civilian personnel and hundreds of contractors funded under a PM Biometrics contract. These contractors issued biometrics equipment to U.S. and Coalition combat units, conducted training for system operators, performed system maintenance and troubleshooting, and operated the biometrics screening systems that controlled access to the larger U.S./Coalition bases.

## WHAT IS THE BEST ORGANIZATIONAL APPROACH?

For most of my biometrics career, I have resisted the notion that the intelligence side should have a primacy over biometrics as opposed to an operationally focused staff element or organization. My concern has always been that if biometrics missions and biometric data became the exclusive purview of the intelligence profession, then the ability to support the kinds of missions I describe here would be severely limited. After all, I know from decades of personal experience that we in the intelligence profession do not always share willingly or play nice with those outside our profession (and often not that well with our professional brothers, either). Data collected, processed, and analyzed by intelligence systems, organizations, and personnel tend to be classified, with dissemination of that information restricted to those with the appropriate clearances and approved need-to-know. I have discussed my concerns with restrictions on the sharing of biometrics data previously and will do so again in Appendix E, but suffice it to say here that biometrics data needs to flow freely to and from those who will be most likely involved in biometrics encounters in the battlespace, and these are, for the most part, not intelligence personnel.

Having said this, in my view we in the DoD have failed to generate a real appreciation for the value of biometrics across conventional combat/ operational force and we have probably come to the point that biometrics as an operational tool is only sustainable if it is treated first and foremost as an intelligence concern. I also believe that the way in which we will collect biometrics data in the future, particularly as the U.S. involvement in Afghanistan winds down, will be much less focused on the direct collection of biometrics from enrollments and much more dependent upon data collected covertly or clandestinely. But making such data available to the conventional force for the kinds of missions I've articulated here (and will discuss more in the following appendix) will require a major technical and procedural shift in how we collect, format, store, and share biometrics and related information, some of which I have described in the book.

In fact, I really like the approach taken by AFRICOM, in which you have the intelligence staff as the lead, but where responsibility for the biometrics and forensic efforts is shared with the operations staff. I think this makes a great deal of sense for a capability such as biometrics, where a fused Ops–Intel approach is necessary to allow us to collect, manage, and use this critical identification data seamlessly across all operational, intelligence, and supporting efforts. Unfortunately, such an integrated concept runs against the antiquated, stove-piped approach that is the current staff organizational model for most militaries.

# APPENDIX E: HOW WE ALMOST CREATED A MULTINATIONAL MILITARY BIOMETRICS DATABASE

My deployment to Afghanistan in 2009 coincided with a major push to expand the use of biometrics across the country, and to incorporate biometrics into operations conducted by all major members of the International Security Assistance Forces (ISAF). Prior to this time, the vast majority of biometrics collections were performed by U.S. forces, or by Coalition forces using U.S.-provided equipment, and operating with and under the control of the U.S. military. Often, the collected data had to be extracted from the collection device and stored on a disc by a member of the U.S. military or a U.S. contractor and then physically transferred to the U.S.-only communications network in order for the data to be submitted for matching. This arrangement obviously resulted in delays in the submission of biometrics collections and occasionally led to situations in which the complete results of the match could not be reported back to the foreign military units that collected it because they contained intelligence information available to U.S. forces only.

For those allied countries that had deployed with their own biometrics collection capabilities, their ability to match those collections against the data in the U.S. ABIS was often severely constrained by their own country's privacy or personal data-sharing laws and policies. These policies caused some ISAF members to restrict the submission of biometric data collected on Afghan citizens to the U.S. ABIS because of their concern that such data would eventually find its way into the hands of the U.S. intelligence community.* In addition, a number of nations were concerned about how they would control the data they collected in Afghanistan after

* I often found it curious that some of our European allies and the Canadians seemed to extend the protections of their national privacy laws to illiterate Afghan villagers, who probably had no such concerns themselves, but such seems to have been the case.

their participation in the ISAF was over. As I have stated, the success of any biometrically-based identification program is dependent upon the ability to share collected data across organizational boundaries, and this was certainly the case in Afghanistan, where the military operation was based upon a wide range of allied nations working together in a coalition.

To help overcome the concerns of many allies about data control and to, hopefully, expand their biometrics collection and sharing efforts, from 2009 to 2010 the BIMA led an effort to develop a regional biometrics data-matching and storage system called ISAF ABIS. This was to be a local database that would, in theory, have allowed each nation to submit biometrics to the system, while maintaining a measure of control over the flow of that data. The concept was that each participating ISAF member would store the data collected by its own forces in a separate partition (or data silo) within the database. Each nation would also establish its own business rules to control with whom (if anyone) they shared their collections, how matches against their data would be performed, and how the results of those matches would be reported. There was also to be an overall policy that each nation could determine the disposition of any data they had collected once their participation in ISAF came to an end.* While such a system was not optimal in that full sharing across the Coalition would probably not have occurred, it was better to have some data collected and shared than none at all. Unfortunately, this capability was never to come to fruition due, in part, to funding constraints. However, the broad concept was fundamentally sound and should be incorporated into the future DoD database, or those of our allies, so that future coalition military operations can be provided with timely biometrics support.

* Countries could choose to leave their data in the system, remove it for their own national use (for homeland security for example), or have it deleted.

# APPENDIX F: COMMON BIOMETRICS AND RELATED TERMINOLOGY

The words and phrases below were taken from a number of documents. I've edited them to be more understandable to the common, nonbiometrics reader, and to fit my own knowledge and experience. You'll note that many do not appear anywhere in the text; however, they are terms you'll often find in other biometrics-related documents, so I've included them here as well.

*Analyze*—Refers to both analysis of the biometrics themselves as well as to the investigatory or intelligence-related process of using biometrics and other information to reach logical conclusions on an individual's identity and actions/intentions. These conclusions can include his intent, affiliation(s), activities, location, and behavioral patterns.

*Associated Information*—Nonbiometric information about a person. For example, a person's name, personal habits, age, current and past addresses, current and past employers, telephone number(s), email address(es), place of birth, family names, nationality, education level, group affiliations, and history, including such characteristics as nationality, educational achievements, employer, security clearances, financial, and credit history. Some of this data may be collected during a biometric enrollment and others may be discovered during analysis, as noted above.

*Authentication*—The process of establishing confidence in the truth of some claim. The claim could be any declarative statement: for example, "This individual's name is 'Joseph K.'" or "This child is more than 5 feet tall." In biometrics, "authentication" is sometimes used as a generic synonym for verification.

*Authoritative Source*—The primary approved repository of biometric information on a biometric subject. The authoritative source provides a strategic capability for access to standardized, comprehensive, and current biometric files within the DoD (Department of Defense) and for sharing of biometric files with joint, interagency and designated multinational partners. Previous BIMA leaders have struggled to define ABIS as the DoD "authoritative source" for biometrics, even though it was noted, as far back as 2007, in a PM Bio White Paper, that this description was inaccurate. In fact there are repositories of biometric data outside of DoD ABIS that their users treat as "authoritative" for their purposes. For example, biometrics for DoD employees is held by the Defense Manpower Data Center in the Defense Enrollment and Eligibility Reporting System (DEERS) database. The BAT database also contains biometrics information not in ABIS.

*Behavioral Biometric*—A biometric characteristic that is learned and acquired over time, rather than one based primarily on biology. Examples of biometric modalities for which behavioral characteristics may dominate, include signature recognition, gait, and keystroke dynamics. A significant amount of study has gone into using behavioral characteristics to determine the intent of an individual. For example, a person's gait may indicate intent to conduct some violent act, or could reflect that they possess some kind of weapon.

*Biological Biometric*—A biometric characteristic based primarily on an anatomical or physiological characteristic, rather than a learned behavior. Examples of biometric modalities for which biological characteristics may dominate, include fingerprint and hand geometry. However, a biological characteristic, such as hair color, age, or sex, could also be used as a "soft biometric" to help determine identity.

*Biometric*—Measurable physical characteristic or personal behavior trait used to recognize the identity or verify the claimed identity of an individual.

*Biometrics Enabled Intelligence*—Intelligence information associated with and or derived from biometrics data that matches a specific person or unknown identity to a place, activity, device, component, or weapon, that supports a terrorist/insurgent network and related pattern analysis, facilitates high-value individual targeting, reveals movement patterns, and confirms claimed identity.

*Biometric File*—The standardized individual dataset resulting from a collection action that consists of a biometric sample and contextual data.

*Biometric Samples*—Information or computer data obtained from a biometric sensor device. Examples are images of a face, or fingerprint.

*Biometrics*—The process of recognizing an individual, based on measurable anatomical, physiological, and behavioral characteristics.

*Collect*—Obtain biometric and related contextual data from an object, system, or individual with, or without, his/her knowledge.

*Contextual Data*—Elements of biographical and situational information (who, what, when, where, how, why, etc.) that are associated with a collection event and permanently recorded as an integral component of the biometric file. The issue of contextual data has complicated the issue of biometrics classification, since certain kinds of contextual data could rightly be considered classified under certain conditions. Examples of this include association a particular collection with a unit, location, and operation name.

*Database*—A collection of one or more computer files. For biometric systems, these files could consist of biometric sensor readings, templates, match results, related end-user information, etc.

*Enrollment*—The process of collecting a biometric sample from an end-user, converting it into a biometric reference, and storing it in the biometric system's database for later comparison. It normally includes collecting contextual and biological/biographical data as well. Enrollments will vary based upon purpose and environment but generally are categorized as follows:

- *Hasty*: A minimum set of biometrics and other data will be collected, which may be specified in a unit SOP or by regional policy. These kinds of enrollment will often occur during actual combat operations, when time is limited.
- *Full/Complete*: A full set of biometrics will be captured, limited only by the capability of the collection device, as well as all contextual and biographical data possible. These will normally occur in a controlled environment, with little time-sensitivity, such as enrollments from hiring or base access, or during the formal detention process.

*Forensics*—Scientific analysis linking persons, places, things, and events. As noted in the text, this is another problematic term for biometrics, since it refers both to a means of collecting and to the analysis of data, both biometric and nonbiometric, for what has historically been a law enforcement role. For biometrics, I prefer to think of forensics as simply a means of collecting a biometric from a historical event, or, as my friend Allen Wight refers to it, "latent biometrics."

*Homeland Security Presidential Directive-24*: A key biometrics-related policy statement that purportedly states how biometrics shall be collected, used, and shared across the USG (U.S. Government). (Note: Like many such high-level authoritative policy documents, HSPD-24 is open to considerable interpretation, is unenforceable, and is essentially an unfunded mandate that has not resulted in sufficient funding to help organizations and agencies implement its provisions.)

**HSPD-24: BIOMETRICS FOR IDENTIFICATION AND SCREENING TO ENHANCE NATIONAL SECURITY**

This directive establishes a framework to ensure that Federal executive departments and agencies use mutually compatible methods and procedures in the collection, storage, use, analysis, and sharing of biometric and associated biographic and contextual information of individuals in a lawful and appropriate manner, while respecting their information privacy and other legal rights under United States law.

*Identification*—A task in which the biometric system searches a database for a reference matching a submitted biometric sample and, if found, returns a corresponding identity. A biometric is collected and compared to all references in a database. Identification is "closed-set" if the person is known to exist in the database. In "open-set" identification, sometimes referred to as a "watchlist," the person is not guaranteed to exist in the database.

*Identity*—The set of attribute values (i.e., characteristics) by which an entity is recognizable and that, within the scope of an identity manager's responsibility, is sufficient to distinguish that entity from any other entity and to distinguish the identity from any other identity. (Note: A word of caution is called for here, as sometimes the concepts of "identity" and "identification" can be a bit misunderstood. For example, as I noted in Chapter 2, "identity" is only as accurate as the data we have to confirm it, which usually occurs the first time we encounter an individual. It is probably less accurate to say that we know *the* identity of an individual in our system than to say we know *an* identity. It's all based on the GIGO principle (i.e., Garbage In, Garbage Out). I believe each identity in our system, or at least those on a watchlist, should have some kind of score, based upon how certain we are of the accuracy of the individual's base identity. This also affects the concept of "identification," which simply means that when I encounter you, I determine that you are the same individual that I encountered before, not that I know who you *really* are.)

*Identity Management*—The combination of technical systems, policies and processes that create, define, govern, and synchronize the ownership, utilization, and safeguarding of identity information.

*Individual*—A specific, physical person.

*Information Assurance*—Operational capabilities that facilitate information sharing, while protecting and defending electronic information and information systems by ensuring their availability, integrity, authentication, and confidentiality.

*Joint Force*—A general term applied to a force comprised of significant elements, assigned or attached, of two or more U.S. Military departments operating under a single Joint Force commander. (Note: This is distinct from a "Combined Force" or "Coalition," which is a military force containing elements from two or more different countries operating under a single commander. An example of this is the International Security Assistance Force (ISAF) in Afghanistan.)

*Latent*—A substance lying dormant or hidden until circumstances are suitable for development or manifestation.

*Liveness Detection*—The ability of a biometrics system to determine that a biometric sample comes from a live person and is not a fake. For example, a fingerprint reader might also have a sensor to detect body heat or to distinguish a real fingerprint from a live person to a fake one made of plastic (or an amputated finger, dependent upon how long it has been since it was severed).

*Local Trusted Source*—A subset of the authoritative source that is established to accomplish a specific function within an operational mission or business function. Reasons for establishing a local trusted source include: insufficient network connectivity able to provide immediate access to the authoritative source, or an operational need for closed-loop access or permission application. If a match is not made against a local trusted source, then the file should be queried against the authoritative source.

*Local Untrusted Source*—A local repository of biometric files that have not been enrolled with an authoritative or local trusted source. In many cases, local untrusted sources are established for missions of short duration or to satisfy political, policy, or legal restrictions related to the sharing of biometric information. An example of this could be a temporary biometrics repository set up to manage humanitarian operations during a natural disaster. The data could be deleted at the end of the operation or ingested into an authoritative source, dependent upon bilateral or multilateral agreements.

*Logical Access*—Process of granting access to information system resources to authorized users, programs, processes, or other systems. The controls and protection mechanisms limit users' access to information and restrict their forms of access to only what is appropriate.

*Match*—A decision that a biometric sample and a stored template comes from the same human source, based on their high level of similarity.

*Modality*—A type or class of biometric system. For example, face recognition, fingerprint recognition, iris recognition, etc.

*Multimodal Biometric System*—A biometric system in which two or more modalities are collected and used for matching. For example, the U.S. ABIS stores facial images, fingerprints, iris image, and palm prints. It can match all but palm.

- *Multimodal biometrics fusion*: The process of matching more than one biometric modality and fusing (combining) the results for a single match score. This can be done in a variety of ways but the bottom line is that the resultant score should be a more accurate indicator of the identification than any single one taken alone. The U.S. ABIS can and has fused face, finger, and iris for matches. There are other "multis" that can be employed to improve match accuracy as well, including
    - *Multi sample*: collecting the same biometric sample (e.g., a single fingerprint) multiple times, matching each, and fusing the results
    - *Multi instance*: collecting variants of the same modality, matching and fusing the results
    - *Multi algorithm*: applying different algorithms to the matching process and fusing the results of each

*Non-DoD Partners*—Interagency and multinational partners.

*Normalize*—Create a standardized, high-quality biometric file consisting of a biometric sample and contextual data. Normalization puts the data in a standardized form and format in order to facilitate the matching process.

*One-to-Many* (1:N)—A phrase used in the biometrics community to describe a system that compares one reference to many enrolled references to make a decision. The phrase typically refers to the *identification* of an individual.

*One-to-One* (1:1)—A phrase used in the biometrics community to describe a system that compares one reference to one enrolled reference to make a decision. The phrase typically refers to the *verification* task (though not all verification tasks are truly one-to-one). For example, an individual comes to an access gate and presents his or her biometric-enabled badge which has the individual's iris template from his/her initial enrollment. The biometrics system scans the badge and extracts the iris template, then scans the individual's "live" iris, and compares the two.

*Person of Interest*—An individual whose identity is of special interest.

*Physical Access*—The process of granting access to installations and facilities.

*Share*—Exchange standardized biometric files and match results among approved DoD, interagency, and international partners, usually governed by laws, policies, or agreements.

*Source*—An approved database and infrastructure that stores biometrics files.

*Store*—Maintain biometric files to make available standardized, current biometric information of individuals, when and where required. Biometric files are initially enrolled and then subsequently updated as part of storing.

*Verification*—A task where a biometric system attempts to confirm an individual's claimed identity by comparing a submitted sample to one or more previously enrolled templates. See "one-to-one" definition.

# BIBLIOGRAPHY


9/11 and Terrorist Travel. Staff Report of the National Commission on Terrorist Attacks Upon the United States. August 21, 2004, Page 68.

Army Memorandum, Subject: Certification (AR 15-6 Investigation of the 800th Military Police Brigade), June 4, 2004.

Biometrics Identity Management Agency, *Annual Report FY10.*

Biometrics Identity Management Agency, *Biometrics Glossary Version 6.0,* April 2012.

Cross Match's SEEK II may have identified Bin Laden, *Homeland Security Newswire,* May 9, 2011, http://www.homelandsecuritynewswire.com/cross-matchs-seek-ii-may-have-identified-bin-laden

Hao, F., Anderson, R. Daugman, J. *Combining Cryptography with Biometrics Effectively,* University of Cambridge Computer Laboratory, Cambridge, United Kingdom. July 2005.

Kaur, G., Verma, C.K. Comparative analysis of biometric modalities, *International Journal of Advanced Research in Computer Science and Software Engineering,* 4(4), 610, April 2014, ISSN: 2277 128X.

Moruza, P. *Intelligence Center Develops Biometrically Enabled Intelligence to Support Warfighter.* January 8, 2013, http://www.army.mil/article/93969/

Nakamura, D. Signer highlights U.S. security uncertainties abroad, *Washington Post* online, December 18, 2013.

National Science and Technology Council (NSTC), Committee on Technology, Committee on Homeland and National Security, Subcommittee on Biometrics, *Biometrics History,* last updated August 7, 2006.

Perera, D. Cheap and Ubiquitous Biometrics Coming, Says Panel, October 28, 2013, http://www.fiercehomelandsecurity.com/story/cheap-and-ubiquitous-biometrics-coming-says-panel/2013-10-28

Planet Biometrics, Professor Developing Biometric Vaccination Registry, October 6, 2014, http://www.planetbiometrics.com/article-details/i/2255/

Shontz, D. *DNA as Part of Identity Management for the Department of Defense,* RAND Corporation, National Defense Research Institute, Santa Monica, CA, 2010.

The PSC Acquisition and Technology Policy Agenda: Transforming for a Future of Improved Performance and Results, Professional Services Council, July 28, 2014.

U.S. Army Field Manual 34-130, *Intelligence Preparation of the Battlefield,* July 8, 1994.

U.S. Government Accounting Office Report to Congressional Requesters, GAO 12-442, *Defense Biometrics: Additional Training for Leaders and More Timely Transmission of Data Could Enhance the Use of Biometrics in Afghanistan,* April 2012.

U.S. Marine Corps Lessons Learned (MCLL) *Newsletter,* 9, page 7, January 2013.

Vrankulj, A. U.S. Marines announce use of Cross Match biometrics in Afghanistan, *Biometric Update,* August 27, 2013, http://www.biometricupdate.com/201308/u-s-marines-announce-use-of-cross-match-biometrics-in-afghanistan

Young, W. *Embassy Security: From the Outside Looking In,* Rand Corporation, 2013.

# INDEX

## C

## J



## K



## L



## M